Key Topics in Educational Psychology

Written by an experienced academic and practitioner, this book offers a clear and accessible introduction to educational psychology.

The book begins by exploring the history of educational psychology, highlighting key figures in its development and the complex and changing relationship between education and psychology. It examines important theories in the field and provides a discussion of the different methodologies researchers use. Importantly, the book goes on to highlight key impacts of the research on current practice and policy, as well as suggesting emerging areas and future directions for the field. In so doing, it offers a self-contained and easily digestible primer for those studying educational psychology and related disciplines.

Key Topics in Educational Psychology is a must-read for undergraduate and postgraduate students of educational psychology, psychology of education, education, and educational studies. It will also be of interest to practitioners in training, particularly those who work in educational settings, including educational psychologists, teachers, therapists, and social workers.

Lisa Marks Woolfson is Emeritus Professor of Psychology at the University of Strathclyde, Glasgow, UK, and was the first Head of its new School of Psychological Sciences and Health. With many years of experience as a professional educational psychologist working with children, families, and educators, she has developed educational psychology learning modules for undergraduates, postgraduates, and for practitioner educational psychologists. Registered with the Health and Care Professions Council, she has written books on educational psychology and published papers in academic journals on frameworks for educational psychology practice and on inclusive education for children with special needs and disabilities.

BPS Key Topics in Psychology
British Psychological Society

Routledge, in partnership with the British Psychological Society (BPS), is pleased to present *BPS Key Topics in Psychology*, a series of short introductory books that focus on a specific field within psychology. Each book is broken down into bitesize chunks to provide a helpful overview of core psychology topics, made clear by a five-part structure: foundations, theories, methodologies, impacts, and emerging areas. Written by active and experienced authors, these essential books encourage students to approach fundamental concepts with confidence and critical thinking.

Books may incorporate student-friendly pedagogies, including tools such as: feature boxes; key terms and definitions; and links to further reading online. Concise yet comprehensive, these books offer a simple and accessible overview of core psychology topics for students looking for a summary of key concepts in the topic, or those new to the area.

Key Topics in Quantitative Research
Paul Christiansen

Key Topics in Coaching Psychology
Rebecca J. Jones and Holly Andrews

Key Topics in Educational Psychology
Lisa Marks Woolfson

For more information about this series, please visit: www.routledge.com/BPS-Key-Topics-in-Psychology/book-series/BPSKTP

Key Topics in Educational Psychology

Lisa Marks Woolfson

LONDON AND NEW YORK

Designed cover image: Getty Images @smartboy10

First published 2026
by Routledge
4 Park Square, Milton Park, Abingdon, Oxon OX14 4RN

and by Routledge
605 Third Avenue, New York, NY 10158

Routledge is an imprint of the Taylor & Francis Group, an informa business

British Library Cataloguing-in-Publication Data
A catalogue record for this book is available from the British Library

ISBN: 9781032691510 (hbk)
ISBN: 9781032691497 (pbk)
ISBN: 9781032691541 (ebk)

DOI: 10.4324/9781032691541

Typeset in Galliard
by Newgen Publishing UK

Access the Support Material: www.routledge.com/9781032691510

For
Richard
Tessa, Eve, Fergal and David
Esther, Seth, Orla, Sylvie, Ted and Raya

And in memory of my parents
Esta and Maurice Marks

Contents

Acknowledgements

Family and friends have contributed their encouragement, love, and support to the writing of this book. They didn't always realise they were doing this. Sometimes this just involved politely listening and looking interested while I explained how the book was progressing, perhaps in more detail than they needed. I'm aware that not everyone finds the writing of a textbook primer an interesting topic for discussion. But I found talking to others about the work in process really helpful. It gave the work a reality beyond me and my laptop, so a huge thank you for this. Additional thanks go to Esther Davis who helped me with some specific queries about appeal to the student reader. Thanks to Dr Tessa Davis for introducing me to communities of practice. And thanks to Esther and to Orla Davis for help in choosing the cover design. Finally, thanks to Dr Richard Woolfson for everything.

Section 1

Key foundations

This section in summary

Chapter 1

- Development of psychology as a new scientific discipline – Wilhelm Wundt's role
- Application of psychology to education – William James, John Dewey, and Edward Thorndike
- Measuring intelligence in children – Alfred Binet and Theodore Simon
- Stages in cognitive development – Jean Piaget
- Psychometrics and the development of UK educational psychology services – Cyril Burt

Chapter 2

- Reciprocal relationship between educational psychology and psychology
- Interdisciplinary or standalone discipline?
- Who is educational psychology for?
- What is educational psychology?

DOI: 10.4324/9781032691541-1

Chapter 1

How did psychology get into education?

This book is about educational psychology, but have you ever wondered how psychology got itself into education which has always been a distinct field of study itself. What business does psychology, with its own theories and methods, have in education? When, why, and how did psychology apply itself to education? This chapter identifies key developments in the foundations of educational psychology as it emerged from the new discipline of psychology and some of the key figures that made it happen.

The new discipline of psychology

Wilhelm Wundt is usually viewed as the first key figure in psychology's path to becoming a distinct academic discipline. He is consequently often referred to as the founder of psychology, so this is a good place to start. Wundt's background was in medicine, having trained in Heidelberg, but medicine didn't seem to hold his interest, and instead, he became increasingly more attracted to the subject of physiology. He studied with Hermann von Helmholtz who was investigating the physiology of the senses. Von Helmholtz succeeded in measuring the speed of nerve impulses in frogs when previously people had thought information transfer through nerve conduction happened so quickly that it couldn't possibly be measured. Von Helmholtz demonstrated that you could indeed measure this. He then went on to measure how long it took people to be aware that a stimulus had touched

DOI: 10.4324/9781032691541-2

their skin. He found that information transfer from sensing a stimulus on the skin, through the nervous system to the brain, was indeed quantifiable.

Wundt then began to see himself rather as a scientific psychologist and began to teach physiological psychology, focusing on internal physiological changes and how these influence our observations. He thought psychology should use the same experimental methods that physiologists used. In 1879, Wundt opened the world's first experimental psychology laboratory at the University of Leipzig. Its emphasis was on physiological psychology. Wundt was interested in applying these physiological experimental methods to the study of psychology, a brand-new field that was emerging from established areas of study such as philosophy, physiology, and physics. This early psychology was focused on measuring mental and perceptual processes. Participants in experiments in Wundt's laboratory were studied responding to visual and auditory stimuli. Apparatus for these studies included rotating discs to make different colours, prisms and lenses, and tuning forks with resonance boxes. Wundt designed special devices to measure reaction time for these mental processes: chronographs, a special pendulum, and a ball that dropped from a variable height. Wundt's students, for example, studied the connection between physical stimuli such as loudness and what noticeable differences in loudness people were able to distinguish (Henri, 1893; Nicolas & Ferrand, 1999).

Students from many countries came to study psychology with Wundt at his innovative laboratory. They then went back to their home countries and set up more than 30 psychology laboratories. More than half of these new laboratories were in the USA, four were in Germany, and two were in England (Henri, 1893). In addition, Wundt produced many scientific papers on his work. In this way, the new discipline of psychology spread from Leipzig. This dissemination of applying experimental methods to study mental processes was Wundt's major impact. It seems he was an excellent teacher and essentially was what we think of nowadays as an 'influencer'. In academic terms, though, we should be aware that he did not develop any theory of psychology or make any novel discoveries that could be taken forward.

From measuring reaction times to applying psychology to education

While Wundt is credited as the 'father' of psychology, his work had little to do with children or education, so he was not the father of educational psychology. The measurement of reaction times which was a favoured scientific method of Wundt's seems a long way from educational psychology and how children learn and behave. Psychology, though, now began to be taught at universities beyond Leipzig in the later part of the 19th century. It was not yet a separate discipline, but rather a component of philosophy or physiology courses. Professors who taught it were not psychologists but instead were professors from other fields who had developed an interest in this new field of study (Fuchs, 2000, 2002). It was William James at Harvard University and John Dewey at the University of Chicago who first extended psychological ideas to teaching and learning in school children.

Online resource 1.1 Wundt's experimental psychology laboratory

UWaterlooPsych380 (2011). Wundt's complication pendulum. 9 Sept. Available at: www.youtube.com/watch?v=Zr7O41r8uEI (Accessed: 28 February 2025)

William James's background and interests were varied. He had trained in medicine but decided not to practise and instead taught anatomy, physiology, and philosophy at Harvard University. He then became interested in psychology and is acknowledged as America's first psychologist and the first person to teach a psychology course at an American university. It was he who was one of the first to have an interest in extending the focus of interest of the new field of psychology to the problems of education. James gave lectures to teachers about applying psychology to teaching and then published the talks in his book *Talks to teachers and to students on some of life's ideals* in 1899. The book, adapted for teachers, incorporates ideas from James's famous 1890 psychology text *Principles of psychology* which had become the leading English language textbook for the study of psychology. *Talks to teachers* has been regularly reprinted and indeed is still in print. It has been translated into many languages including Russian, demonstrating the popularity of its ideas across time and across cultures, as well as its relevance to the theory of education. James showed teachers how psychological concepts such as memory and reasoning could usefully be applied to education (Brysbaert & Rastle, 2009; Myers, 2001).

John Dewey was an educator and philosopher who founded a pioneering Laboratory School at the University of Chicago, in 1894. The school began with one teacher and twelve pupils and grew within a few years to over one hundred children. It was an experimental school that was set up to allow Dewey to research innovations in teaching methods. His aim was to test out and evaluate new curricula and progressive ideas about how children learn. Bear in mind that whole-class teaching in large classes, and rote recall as evidence of learning, were traditional approaches to education at that time. But Dewey thought that children learned by experience, by 'doing' rather than by being told. He applied new psychological ideas about the developing child to re-characterise education as individual, child-centred, and experiential. Rather than being didactic instructors delivering knowledge or strict disciplinarians ensuring children learned to sit quietly and listen, Dewey's teachers adopted a new role as facilitators of children's learning and organisers of suitable learning experiences. This became known as the progressive education movement (Pring, 2014).

Online resource 1.2 John Dewey: philosophy of education
Sprouts. (2021). John Dewey's four principles of education. 30 January. Available at: www.youtube.com/watch?v=y3fm6wNzK70 (Accessed: 28 February 2025)

Emergence of educational psychology

Edward Thorndike was one of William James's students at Harvard University. When he was an undergraduate student, Thorndike had read James's book, *Principles of psychology*, and was excited by the idea of psychology evolving as an empirical discipline. He decided to learn more about this by studying under James at Harvard. Thorndike became interested in applying psychology to understanding how children learn. This was the beginning of psychology's interest in learning. Subsequently, during his long career as a professor at Columbia University, Thorndike produced over 500 influential papers on educational psychology.

As it was not always easy to recruit children to study learning, Thorndike instead often research learning behaviour in animals. He did this by observing and recording the animals' behaviour under controlled conditions. A famous set of studies involved a puzzle box, a wooden crate where hungry animals, dogs, chickens, and especially cats, learned to pull a string or a lever to open a door and get themselves out of the box to access food. Thorndike noted that at first solving this puzzle took a while but that it took the animals less and less time on repeated trials. He explained that the cats, at first, acted instinctively and irrelevantly, for example, hissing and swinging their paws. Eventually, one of their actions by chance would lead to pulling the string and opening the door to the food. This was the law of effect, an important principle in the theory of **behaviourism**, where animals learned to stop using behaviours that were unsuccessful in opening the door but rather repeat those that had achieved the outcome of solving the puzzle to get to the food. The cats now associated the stimulus of being in the puzzle box with the successful response for opening the door. They had learned to open the door through their experience of being in the box.

Behaviourism Theory of learning that views behaviours as being learned through reinforcement by environmental stimuli.

In 1906, Thorndike published a book *The principles of teaching based upon psychology*. His insights into the science of learning suggested it was the responsibility of the teacher to provide instructional experiences that would result in children's learning, rather than it being the child's responsibility to absorb knowledge themselves (Brysbaert & Rastle, 2009; Mayer, 2014).

While Wundt is usually viewed as the 'founder of psychology', Thorndike is seen as the 'founder of educational psychology' and acknowledged as the main person who changed the focus of study of education from philosophy to psychological science. The application of psychology to educational practice was now well under way.

Online resource 1.3 Thorndike's puzzle box
Stienissen, G. (2010). *Puzzle box (Thorndike)*. 19 August. Available at: www.youtube.com/watch?v=fanm--WyQJo (Accessed: 28 February 2025).

Measuring intelligence in children: individual psychology

Alfred Binet During the 1880s, an elementary school education became compulsory for children in several countries, including the UK and the USA. It was felt, however, that regular education might not be suitable for all children and that special education should be provided for children with, what we now refer to as, special needs and disabilities. In France in 1904, Alfred Binet was appointed to a government commission tasked with exploring the issue of identifying which children special education would be more suitable for.

Binet had trained in law and then medicine but became more interested in the new psychology. He worked for 6 years at Salpêtrière Hospital in Paris, a centre of excellence in psychology, assisting Jean-Martin Charcot, a famous neurologist and psychiatrist. He followed this by spending time at home studying child development through his own daughters' reaction times, sensory perception, and number concepts.

France's only experimental psychology laboratory had been established by Henri Beaunis at the Sorbonne in Paris, following the same model as Wundt's Leipzig Institute (Carroy & Schmidgen, 2004). Binet took an unpaid position there carrying out extensive psychological research, including studying memory in children. He joined a society for educational research which regularly published articles of practical relevance to teachers, eventually becoming the society's leader. Theodore Simon, a young medical student who had professional connections with children with learning difficulties, was also a member of the society (Fancher, 2013).

Binet and Simon worked together to address the problem of which children would benefit from a special education programme, rather than from regular education. Binet became aware that the popular **psychometric** measure of reaction time was not a satisfactory tool for distinguishing between children with learning difficulties and those without, between children of different levels of 'intelligence'. Similarly, they realised that measures of perceptions and sensations as carried out in the new experimental psychology labs did not achieve the task either, and nor did anthropomorphic measures of the size of children's heads, despite the belief at that time that a small head indicated poor abilities.

Psychometric Measurement of mental processes. Psychometric methods refer to assessment, evaluation, questionnaires, and testing procedures designed to measure aspects of human performance and behaviour including intelligence.

In 1904, Binet carried out a study in which children were asked to learn a poem and then later show what they remembered of it. Able pupils as identified by teachers performed better on this task than less able pupils. Binet and Simon saw that items related to intellectual activities rather than to laboratory tasks better achieved the purpose of differentiating those children with learning difficulties. Through focusing on 'higher functions', more complex activities such as memory, abstract thinking, reasoning, and understanding, they built up a picture of which cognitive tasks children of different ages could carry out successfully. This was a new area of psychology, individual psychology, the study of individual differences in psychological processes (Brysbaert & Rastle, 2009; Mülberger, 2017; Nicolas et al., 2014).

Box 1.1 Case study: how Binet and Simon developed their intelligence test

Alfred Binet was given the task of identifying which children would not be suited to regular education which had recently become compulsory in France. These children were to be provided with suitable special education, but it was strongly felt that there needed to be a method for categorising children in this way. Neither reaction times nor anthropometric measures were useful for this.

Binet and his colleague Theodore Simon carried out lengthy studies with children of different ages in the Salpêtrière Hospital and then in primary schools in Paris. They used simple, quick tests in a continuous sequence aiming for these to last about 20 minutes as they felt that any longer would tire the child. They were very clear that they wanted to evaluate intelligence independent from what the child had been taught in school. They didn't ask children to read or write anything. They were aiming to assess what they perceived as 'natural intelligence'.

Binet and Simon were also explicit about testing being in a quiet room and how the examiner should encourage the child but without making suggestions as to how to answer the questions. Tests began with those appropriate to the child's age so that they were neither too difficult nor too easy at first. Binet and Simon classified their tests according to the ages at which most children managed to succeed on them, so a 'normal' 5-year-old could copy a square, put together a two-piece figure, and count four coins. A 10-year-old could name the months of the year and answer comprehension questions.

They recognised that children would be able to successfully carry out some tests for older age groups. They arranged the tests in order of increasing difficulty, having established this order through their many trials. Their principle was that if children succeeded in all but one of the tests of a particular age group, they were viewed as having the intellectual level of that age group. If the child was able to pass tests of older age groups they were seen as advanced. If they did not succeed in passing tests for their age group, then regular schooling might not be suitable.

Binet, A., & Simon, T. (1961). The development of intelligence in children. In J.J. Jenkins & D.G. Paterson (Eds.), *Studies in individual differences: The search for intelligence* (pp. 81–111). Appleton-Century-Crofts.

In 1907, Binet and Simon's work resulted in the first validated intelligence test with **standardised norms** that reflected the items that children of different ages could be expected to succeed at and which did not principally depend on what the children were learning at school (Arnold & Leadbetter, 2013; Fancher, 2013). In what has been described as 'genius' and a significant contribution to psychology (Anderson, 2017; Miller, 1984), Binet and Simon developed the concept of mental age based on children's performance on the test. A child's mental age could be compared to children's chronological age to identify the extent of the child's difficulties and therefore suitability for regular or special education.

Standardised norms Scales with data for comparison of individual's test performance with typical performance for children of the same age.

Online resource 1.4 Binet and intelligence testing
Smith, P. (2012). *Alfred Binet and intelligence testing.* 7 August. Available at: www.youtube.com/watch?v=9KEAow2cTIk (Accessed: 28 February 2025).

Critical thinking task 1.1

Some educators question the value of intelligence testing.
What information is gained from intelligence testing?
How might educators apply this new information in the classroom?

Cognitive development

Jean Piaget, a Swiss psychologist, began working as a research assistant in Binet and Simon's laboratory after Binet's death. His job was to standardise the French version of a newly developed reasoning test. What Piaget became really interested in was not the right or wrong answers that children gave to the test questions, but instead he wanted to know more about their explanations for reaching these answers. By questioning the children about the reasoning for their answers, particularly about incorrect answers, he learned much about how children think differently and interpret the world differently from adults (Brainerd, 1996).

Piaget studied **cognitive development** to explain how children acquire important concepts by developing their understandings through different ages and stages of their lives. His output was prodigious, and his ideas have influenced the research of psychologists after him right up to the present day. This makes it a challenge to select significant achievements. Stage theory, one of his key contributions to the area of educational psychology, is presented here on the understanding that there are many more. More of Piaget's ideas and how they have been taken forward in educational psychology, as well as how they have been critiqued, will be examined in Chapter 3 when we consider key theories of child development.

Cognitive development Process of change in children as their thinking grows and matures. Change can be gradual or a more abrupt transition from one stage of thinking to the next.

Stage theory

Piaget proposed that children's cognitive (intellectual) development progressed through four stages roughly corresponding to the ages in brackets:

Sensorimotor period (from birth to 2 years) During this first period the young child's awareness of objects depends on sensation, seeing, touching, and mouthing an object. This is how the child learns about a toy, and when not connecting with the toy through senses, the child is not aware that it is still there. This is referred to as the child lacking understanding of **object permanence** that the toy is still there; it still exists, even when the child cannot see or touch it.

Object permanence Baby at about 8 months old understands that an object exists and is permanent and that a toy still exists even when the baby can't see it because it is covered up.

Pre-operational period (2–7 years) Preschool children and early years infants do not understand mental operations such as conservation of quantity. The child understands that two identical tumblers hold the same quantity of liquid. But when all the liquid from one of those tumblers is poured into a taller, narrower glass, pre-operational children think this glass now has more liquid, even though they know no more has been added.

Concrete operational period (7–11 years) Older primary-aged children understand conservation of quantity. They know that if the glass is taller and looks bigger, the dimension of the glass's width compensates for this. Concrete operational children can manipulate two dimensions to make this judgement correctly. However, they can only deal with concrete ideas, not abstract thinking.

Formal operational period (11 years through adolescence) This stage is characterised by logical thinking and the ability to tackle hypothetical problems. It is seen in secondary school-aged children.

Online resource 1.5 Piaget's theory of cognitive development
Sprouts. (2018). *Piaget's theory of cognitive development*. 1 August. Available at: www.youtube.com/watch?v=IhcgYgx7aAA (Accessed: 28 February 2025).

You can see that Piaget's idea of stages explains very well for educators how children need to be ready to understand different concepts by progressing through these different stages. It is commonly accepted in education, for example, that children will best learn abstract concepts about numbers, if they first have had concrete experience of manipulating numbers of items themselves. This is in preference to just having the concept explained abstractly to them.

Development of professional educational psychology service in the UK

Cyril Burt was both a significant and a controversial figure in the growth of the discipline of educational psychology. We noted that in the early stages of his career, Piaget worked on a French version

Box 1.2 Case study: learning from your children – Binet and Piaget

Both Alfred Binet and Jean Piaget developed their cutting-edge theories about children's intelligence from initially observing their own children at home.

Binet gave his two daughters, Madeleine (5 years) and Alice (3 years), tests of reaction time and sensory acuity and published his findings. He found that they were similar to adults in judging lengths of lines and acuteness of angles but were slower in responding than adults and inconsistent compared to adults because of loss of attention to the task. Binet concluded that children's sensory abilities, while similar to those of adults, differ in other ways. This influenced his later development of intelligence testing as he realised that sensory tests did not usefully discriminate intellectual ability. Binet also tested Madeleine on what post-Piaget we recognise as conservation of quantity, with Madeleine incorrectly judging 10 large tokens to be more than 18 small tokens (Fancher, 2013).

Piaget tested and observed his three children, Jacqueline, Laurent, and Lucienne extensively, typically several times a day. He and his wife Valentine, also a psychologist, recorded what they witnessed in diaries and formulated theories based on their interpretation of how the young children interacted with and learned about their environment. Because it was Piaget's own children, it was easier for him to gain longitudinal data as the children grew older. Piaget first presented their theory of infant development to the British Psychological Society in 1927. For example, Piaget described 10-month-old Laurent searching for his toy when he saw it being hidden under a pillow. Before that, he searched inconsistently because he did not have the concept of **object permanence** that the toy still exists even when he can't see it. Piaget noted that peekaboo with an adult hiding was different for infants and that they enjoy this game and know the hidden adult still exists, earlier than they understand a hidden toy still exists (Fischer & Hencke, 1996).

of a reasoning test. That reasoning test was developed by Cyril Burt, who was the first, and for many years the only, educational psychologist in the UK. Burt was appointed to this role in 1913 by London County Council. He was invited to write his own terms of reference for the post which he viewed as a scientist-practitioner within the field of education. He saw the role as involving both practical work assessing individual children who had learning or behaviour problems in schools or were gifted, but also as involving carrying out research studying children. Burt worked both with individual children and more broadly in the area of curriculum development as well as devising the instruments needed for the tasks. He also established the first UK training programme for practitioner educational psychologists (Maliphant et al., 2013).

Critical thinking task 1.2

You might like to explore how educational psychologists are currently trained in UK by checking out the British Psychological Society website www.bps.org.uk/educational-psychologist-job-profile
How does the role of the modern educational psychologist compare to Burt's 1913 role?

Burt was not only an educational psychologist but also a statistician with specific interest in factor analysis and in creating standardised age norms for the comparison of individual's performance with typical performance for children of the same age. The Burt Word Reading Test, Burt Spelling Test, Northumberland arithmetic and English tests, Moray House Tests, and the 11+ examination for selection and streaming prior to secondary school entry are all examples of standardised tests that Burt had a greater or lesser role in devising and that have been used extensively within the UK education community. Burt also carried out a revision of Binet's scales for UK children. Like Binet, Burt worked on reliable methods of testing to identify children for whom special education was recommended. Unlike Binet though, who thought intelligence was not fixed, Burt's view was that it was fixed and inherited and that there was a link between poverty and intelligence.

Controversy Burt's interest in the heritability of intelligence led to his gathering data from identical twins who had grown up in different households. If intelligence measurements were similar for the separated twins, this suggested a large inherited, genetic component. There began to be debate over the high correlations of .771 Burt reported for the 53 pairs of twins in the study. Additionally, there were queries about how such a high number of separated twins could even have been recruited for the research. Allegations were made that Burt fabricated his data and that Jane Conway and Margaret Howard, the research assistants who were said to have worked on data collection, did not exist. By the 1980s, it was accepted that Burt was guilty of data fabrication and that the twin study data were not reliable. Question marks over Burt's data similarly called into question other standardised norms he developed that were used extensively by educational psychologists. However, 10 years later the research assistants were 'found', and later twin studies found similar correlations to those of Burt (Rushton, 2002).

Change in focus of professional practice of educational psychology From the time of the first educational psychologist to the late 1970s, practitioner educational psychologists supported schools by **psychometric**, **diagnostic**, **remedial**, and **therapeutic** work with individual children. In 1978, however, the publication of a groundbreaking text (Gillham, 1978) stimulated a seminal paradigm shift away from this within-child deficit approach to advocating that it was more

Diagnostic Diagnostic tests focus on identifying children's difficulties, for example, in reading, with a view to offering remediation activities, that is, teaching to improve the problem.

Remedial Remedial education is a term that was used until the 1980s to describe teaching activities that were designed to help slower learners catch up in the basic academic skills.

Therapeutic Early practitioner educational psychologists provided support to children who had emotional difficulties, often making use of play therapy.

effective for practitioner educational psychologists to investigate difficulties not only through traditional within-child psychometric assessment but also to examine the interplay between these difficulties and the social contexts of the school and the home.

Summary

This chapter examined the relationship between education and psychology and how it developed into the new discipline of educational psychology. It showed how, over the course of the 19th and 20th centuries, the influence of far-sighted visionaries from different disciplines, such as Wundt, James, Thorndike, Binet and Simon, and Piaget, and Burt, extended ideas from the new discipline of psychology to help us better understand children's learning and how best to support and facilitate this. Principles of educational psychology became embedded in professional training for educators, in their classroom practice as well as in school policies and wider district and government education policies.

References/Further reading

Anderson, M. (2017). Binet's error: Developmental change and individual differences in intelligence are related to different mechanisms. *Journal of Intelligence*, *5*(2), 24.

Arnold, C., & Leadbetter, J. (2013). A hundred years of applied psychology. *The Psychologist*, *26*(9), 696–698.

Brainerd, C. (1996). Piaget: A centennial celebration. *Psychological Science*, *7*(4), 191–195.

Brysbaert, M., & Rastle, K. (2009). *Historical and conceptual issues in psychology*. Prentice Hall/Pearson Education.

Carroy, J., & Schmidgen, H. (2004). Reaction time tests in Leipzig, Paris and Würzburg. The Franco-German history of a psychological experiment, 1890–1910. *Medizinhistorisches Journal*, *39*(1), 27–55.

Fancher, R. E. (2013). Alfred Binet, general psychologist. *Portraits of pioneers in psychology*, *3*, 67–83.

Fischer, K. W., & Hencke, R. W. (1996). Infants' construction of actions in context: Piaget's contribution to research on early development. *Psychological Science*, *7*(4), 204–210.

Fuchs, A. H. (2000). Teaching the introductory course in psychology circa 1900. *American Psychologist*, *55*(5), 492.

Fuchs, A. H. (2002). *Contributions of American mental philosophers to psychology in the United States*. American Psychological Association.
Gillham, B. (Ed.). (1978). *Reconstructing educational psychology*. Croom Helm.
Henri, V. (1893). Laboratories of experimental psychology in Germany. *Revue Philosophique de la France et de l'Etranger*, *36*, 608–622.
Maliphant, R., Cline, T., & Frederickson, N. (2013). Educational psychology practice and training: The legacy of Burt's appointment with the London County Council. *Educational and Child Psychology*, *30*(3), 46–59.
Mayer, R. E. (2014). EL Thorndike's enduring contributions to educational psychology. In B. Zimmerman and D. Schunk (Eds.), *Educational Psychology: A Century of Contributions: A Project of Division 15* (Educational Psychology) of the American Psychological Society (pp. 113–155). Routledge.
Miller, G. A. (1984). The test; Alfred Binet's method of identifying subnormal schoolchildren sired the IQ test [Article]. *Science '84*, *5*, 55+.
Mülberger, A. (2017). Mental association: Testing individual differences before Binet. *Journal of the History of the Behavioral Sciences*, *53*(2), 176–198.
Myers, G. E. (2001). *William James: His life and thought*. Yale University Press.
Nicolas, S., Coubart, A., & Lubart, T. (2014). The program of individual psychology (1895–1896) by Alfred Binet and Victor Henri. *L'Année psychologique*, *114*(1), 5–60.
Nicolas, S., & Ferrand, L. (1999). Wundt's laboratory at Leipzig in 1891. *History of Psychology*, *2*(3), 194.
Pring, R. (2014). *John Dewey*. Bloomsbury Publishing.
Rushton, J. P. (2002). New evidence on Sir Cyril Burt: His 1964 speech to the Association of Educational Psychologists. *Intelligence*, *30*(6), 555–567.

Chapter 2

What is educational psychology? Who is it for?

Educational psychology and its relationship with psychology

A traditional view of educational psychology is that it is a sub-discipline of psychology, applying theories of psychology to problems in the development and education of children. So educational psychology may be considered as the application of theories of social psychology, cognitive psychology, developmental psychology, and clinical and health psychology to the educational setting (Marks Woolfson, 2011; Slavin, 2018; Wittrock, 1992; Woolfolk Hoy, 2000). According to this view, psychology develops theories, and educational psychology is the recipient of these psychological theories to provide insight into pupils' underlying cognitive, social, emotional, and behavioural functioning in order to improve children's learning and emotional wellbeing.

We saw examples of this one-way relationship in Chapter 1 where the new field of psychology developed theories and measurement tools, and educational psychology acted as an end user of these, applying findings from the psychology research laboratory to children in classrooms. Early educational psychology research was restricted to examining variables such as intelligence and motivation and small components of the learning process such as handwriting, which could be assessed and measured on a scale (O'Donnell & Levin, 2003). This focus on tiny measurable variables resulted in a perception among educators and practitioners that academic educational psychology research was too detached, too theoretical, and reductionist in its approach. Education professionals felt that the study of these variables did not provide them

DOI: 10.4324/9781032691541-3

with practical findings that they could apply to the complex situation of children's learning and behaviour in the social context of the school classroom. Its focus was on the psychological study of children's learning when what educators wanted was research that studied the influence of their teaching on that learning (Veldman & Brophy, 1974).

Importantly though, the relationship between psychology and educational psychology need not be characterised as only one way. In their educational psychology research, Dewey, James, Thorndike, and Binet made seminal contributions to progress our understanding of learning, behaviour, individual differences, thinking, and test measurement. Their work with children resulted in methodologies, concepts, theories, and findings that were adopted by and benefited psychology research beyond that of children and classrooms (Wittrock, 1992). Thus, while psychological ideas were applied to the field of educational psychology, new insights for the wider field of psychology were emerging from research into the psychological study of problems in education. Instead of psychology theories only being handed down for educational psychology to apply, it is more accurate to recognise a reciprocal relationship with original and groundbreaking findings travelling in both directions.

Who is educational psychology for?

Different audiences are looking for different information from educational psychology. There are at least four separate audiences who are interested: education staff, parents and carers, academic researchers, and practitioner educational psychologists.

Educators in schools want practical guidance for classroom problems they face in their work. This group includes not only classroom teachers but also other education professionals such as teaching assistants, emotional literacy support assistants, special educational needs coordinators (SENCOs), learning and behaviour support staff, education mental health practitioners, and nursery nurses. They want to know how best to deal with a child who won't stay in their seat, how to help with a child whose reading is behind the rest of the class, and how to support a child experiencing anxiety in the classroom. And in their position in the frontline of the classroom, they need immediate answers as they must handle these issues right now.

Parents and carers too are interested in the findings of educational psychology research. Like teachers, they are on the frontline, seeking immediate answers to concerns about their children's development, mental health, and behaviour within the family. They may seek psychological advice on online parenting websites, social media, print books, and magazines where writers have distilled educational psychology research findings to be easily accessible.

Theorists and researchers are more concerned with theoretical explanations of psychological processes underlying learning that they can test. Academics and researchers want books and papers that develop and test out theories to explain psychological processes underlying learning. This is quite different from what teachers and education support staff need in the here and now of the classroom.

Practitioner educational psychologists deal with learning and behaviour difficulties, child mental health, social and emotional problems, children with special needs and disabilities and complex developmental problems, vulnerable young people, refugees, and children who have experienced trauma in the age range 0–25 years. They observe children in the classroom, and they interview children and the adults who know them best, carrying out assessment, undertaking consultation, providing advice, and delivering interventions. Practitioner educational psychologists need theory and evidence-informed advice for intervention so that they can offer optimal support and best practice to parents, carers, educators, children and young people, and the wider community.

While these separate groups of educators, researchers, parents/carers, and educational psychologists seek different types of information, they are not operating in silos completely isolated from each other. There is extensive collaboration across their role boundaries. Educational psychologists view themselves as scientist-practitioners. They are involved in training those working with children, in parent education, and in carrying out research. Academic researchers consistently present their findings to end users such as teachers, psychologists, and parents and explain their implications for intervention, classroom practice, or parenting. Teaching staff, educational psychologists, and parents work closely together on jointly finding solutions to children's problems, bringing together their different understandings of the issues.

Is educational psychology an interdisciplinary subject or a standalone discipline?

Interdisciplinary work is where distinctive concepts, language, methods, and knowledge bases of separate disciplines are integrated across their subject boundaries to investigate phenomena of interest to each discipline (Faber & Scheper, 1997). There has been a kind of snobbery about this. A pure, standalone, specialised discipline was sometimes viewed as academically superior to an interdisciplinary 'hybrid' subject. On the other hand, though, there is now recognition that interdisciplinary collaboration is necessary to examine society's challenging problems and that a single disciplinary focus may be too narrow and not sufficient to provide comprehensive insights and inspired solutions (Buyalskaya et al., 2021).

Educational psychology is ahead of the curve here as it has always been an interdisciplinary subject. It grew from interdisciplinary roots in its early beginnings when philosophers, doctors, and mathematicians came together for rigorous investigation of teaching and learning in schools (Alexander, 2018). Over time, it integrated psychology specialties such as learning, motivation, and cognition. These research areas operated quite separately from each other, adopting different theoretical paradigms and publishing their results in different academic journals (Harris, 2018).

Modern educational psychology today brings together problems and issues in education with key insights not only from developmental, clinical, health, cognitive, and social psychology but also from sociology, neuroscience, linguistics, cultural studies, systems theory, and others. This openness of educational psychology to cross-disciplinary fertilisation may be considered a strength that facilitates cutting-edge insights into children's experiences in schools.

As it develops and achieves recognition, an interdisciplinary subject can then become a distinct field in its own right. Even 'pure' subjects like physics developed from interdisciplinary combinations of mathematics, natural philosophy, astronomy, and logic. Neuroscience may be viewed as comprising several underlying disciplines, for example, neurology, psychology, biology, and medicine. Yet both physics and neuroscience are now considered discrete disciplines with their specific bodies of knowledge.

What then is educational psychology?

Educational psychology has now reached the point of being recognised as a discipline in its own right. Its constituent disciplines have now merged to form a unique holistic domain of study. Educational psychology's unifying theme is its focus on the scientific study of children and young people in school, along with the actions of associated adults, not only at the level of the individual, but also at the contextual level of the class, school, or school district.

Educational psychology is the scientific study of education, building a scientific evidence base for the implementation of interventions, through which it develops its own theoretical models and conceptual frameworks (Wittrock, 1992). From its early beginnings, educational psychology has adopted a social justice agenda with its research and interventions aiming to address inequality and reduce disadvantage, for example, identifying and supporting struggling learners to develop literacy skills. This focus on problems that are unique to that discipline, with its distinctive models, research methodology, and inclusive ethos, suggests contemporary educational psychology is now indeed an independent domain, a standalone discipline.

In the UK, 'educational psychology' can refer to both professional work in schools and also academic research. Many UK courses use titles like *Psychology in Education*, *Psychology and Education*, *Psychology of Education* instead of *Educational Psychology*, to signal that students will study academic educational psychology and that the course does not train participants to be professional educational psychologists. In the USA, there is a distinction in the terminology used for researchers and practitioners, with practitioners usually referred to as school psychologists. In this book, the term 'educational psychology' will be used to refer to academic research and evidence-informed application of psychological principles in schools. The terms **practitioner educational psychologist** or **professional educational psychologist** will be used for school psychologists carrying out applied work with schools and families.

Practitioner/professional educational psychologist School psychologist who carries out applied work with children, school staff, carers, and families. This might be at the level of the individual child, the family, the classroom, the school, or the school district.

Summary

This chapter highlighted the complex nature of the relationship between educational psychology and psychology. It explained educational psychology's current focus and discussed the extent to which it may be considered a sub-discipline of psychology, interdisciplinary, or a distinct domain of study. It considered the diverse needs of different audiences for educational psychology research. It clarified that for the purposes of this book the term 'educational psychology' will refer to both academic research and professional practice in educational psychology.

References/Further reading

Alexander, P. (2018). Past as prologue: Educational psychology's legacy and progeny. *Journal of Educational Psychology*, *110*(2), 147–162.

Buyalskaya, A., Gallo, M., & Camerer, C. F. (2021). The golden age of social science. *Proceedings of the National Academy of Sciences*, *118*(5), e2002923118.

Faber, J., & Scheper, W. J. (1997). Interdisciplinary social science: A methodological analysis. *Quality and Quantity*, *31*(1), 37–56.

Harris, K. R. (2018). Educational psychology: a future retrospective. *Journal of Educational Psychology*, *110*(2), 163–173. https://doi.org/10.1037/edu0000267

Marks Woolfson, L. (2011). *Educational psychology: The impact of psychological research on education*. Pearson.

O'Donnell, A. M., & Levin, J. R. (2003). Educational psychology's healthy growing pains. In *Educational Psychology* (pp. 73–82). Routledge.

Slavin, R. E. (2018). *Educational psychology: Theory and practice*. Pearson.

Veldman, D. J., & Brophy, J. E. (1974). Measuring teacher effects on pupil achievement. *Journal of Educational Psychology*, *66*(3), 319.

Wittrock, M. C. (1992). An empowering conception of educational psychology. *Educational Psychologist*, *27*(2), 129–141. https://doi.org/10.1207/s15326985ep2702_1

Woolfolk Hoy, A. (2000). Educational psychology in teacher education. *Educational Psychologist*, *35*(4), 257–270. https://doi.org/10.1207/S15326985EP3504_04

Section 2

Key theories

This section in summary

Chapter 3

- Theories of intelligence
  - o Psychometric
  - o General intelligence *g* and hierarchical models of intelligence
  - o Triarchic theory of successful intelligence
  - o Multiple intelligences
- Cognitive development – young children's understanding of conservation of number
- Criticisms of stage theory
- Theoretical approaches to understanding reading skills

Chapter 4

- Scaffolding
  - o Social constructivist theory – Vygotsky and Bruner
  - o Dynamic assessment – Feuerstein
- Social learning and social cognitive theory – Bandura
- Attribution theory – Weiner
- Attachment theory
- Wider social context
  - o Social ecological theory – Bronfenbrenner
  - o Biopsychosocial model

DOI: 10.4324/9781032691541-4

Chapter 5

- Bullying and cyberbullying – definition and prevalence
- Psychosocial theories applied to bullying
  - Social learning and social cognitive
  - Participant role
  - Social information processing
  - Theory of mind
  - Social identity theory
  - Social dominance theory
  - Theory of planned behaviour

Chapter 6

- Humanistic psychology
- Positive psychology
- Solution-focused psychology

Chapter 3

Child-focused theories in the classroom

Theories of intelligence

This chapter outlines some key theories that help educators understand learning at the level of the individual child. It describes theories of intelligence: Binet's psychometric, Spearman's general intelligence, Cattell's hierarchical model, Sternberg's triarchic model and Gardner's multiple intelligences. Piaget's ideas about conservation of number will be discussed, along with critical evaluation of his concept of 'stage'. The chapter will also consider theories explaining how beginning readers learn to recognise words.

Psychometric theories

In Chapter 1, we saw why and how Binet and Simon developed their test for measuring intelligence in children. Underlying Binet's approach was his belief that intellectual abilities developed and changed according to age and environmental opportunities and that intelligence was not fixed. The key point here is that Binet viewed intelligence as an entity that was able to be measured by evaluating the ability to perform well in a variety of different tasks, tasks that did not rely on class lessons. This is a **psychometric** theory of intelligence where intelligence is considered measurable by a series of tests.

Psychometric Measurement of mental processes. Psychometric methods refer to assessment, evaluation, questionnaires, and testing procedures designed to measure aspects of human performance and behaviour including intelligence.

Using the intelligence scales that he

DOI: 10.4324/9781032691541-5

developed, Binet calculated the child's mental age and compared it to chronological age to determine which children needed extra help in their education. It was William Stern, a German psychologist, who modified this by proposing that rather than considering the difference between mental age and chronological age, a new concept, the intelligence quotient (IQ), could be used. (Kovacs & Pléh, 2023). Stern's formula was simple:

> **Mental age** Mental ability age as calculated by performance on standardised intelligence test.

> **Chronological age** This is how old you are as measured in years and months from birth.

IQ = **mental age** as measured by psychometric test divided by the child's **chronological age**.

If the child's mental age was at the level of their chronological age, IQ would be 1. If the child was advanced, IQ would be greater than 1, and if their intelligence was at the level of a child younger than their age, the quotient would be less than 1. IQ subsequently became one of educational psychology's most recognised and enduring concepts. Even more modern tests that do not use this mental age/chronological age to report their scores are still referred to as IQ tests. Indeed, in common usage, 'IQ' is regularly used as a proxy term for intelligence, even where a series of measurable tasks have not been carried out.

It was Lewis Terman, an American psychologist, who further simplified the IQ score to the one we recognise today by multiplying the mental/chronological age formula by 100. IQ would be 100 if mental age was at the same level as chronological age, that is, average. If the child's intelligence was measured at the level of a child younger than their age, it would be a number below 100 which is simpler to work with than a fraction less than 1. An advanced IQ score would be greater than 100. Terman, working at Stanford University, revised the test for use with American children and named it the Stanford-Binet test of intelligence. You will note that Simon's name was now lost from the credits for this work.

General intelligence (g)

Our early understanding of intelligence was largely defined by performance on these scales. Those who performed well on the items on the scales achieved a high IQ score and therefore were considered to be intelligent (Hunt, 1983). A key underlying assumption of Binet, Simon, and Terman's work on developing their scales was that they were measuring general intelligence, a single ability. Charles Spearman in 1904 used statistical methods to demonstrate there was indeed some consistency in children's successful performance on intelligence tests and in different school subjects. Using factor analysis, he found there was a common general factor across tests of mental abilities, which he referred to as *g*, **general intelligence**.

General intelligence (g) Through factor analysis, Charles Spearman found common general factor across tests of mental abilities. He referred to this as *g*, general intelligence.

Hierarchical models of intelligence

In addition, Spearman recognised that specialised skills also explain some smaller part of the variance in performance in different tasks on IQ tests. This is a two-factor theory with factors of general intelligence, *g*, and specific abilities. A **hierarchical theory of intelligence** refers to there being different levels of abilities that contribute to performance on intellectual tasks. General intelligence (*g*) is at the top of the hierarchy, at the highest level, as it contributes the most. Specialised mathematical or language or spatial abilities are at a lower level than *g* as they make an important but lesser contribution to specific individual tasks. For example, if a child does well in a vocabulary test, much of that is because of *g*, but some smaller part is because of the child's specific language skills.

Hierarchical theory of intelligence Different levels of abilities that contribute to performance on intellectual tasks with *g* at the highest level.

Raymond Cattell's psychometric analyses of tests with adults led him to a different two-factor theory. He proposed instead that intelligence is comprised of fluid intelligence, the ability to solve problems flexibly, to analyse and reason your way through new situations, and crystallised intelligence, knowledge learned through education and built up over the years (Cattell, 1943). His theory was further developed and refined by Horn and Carroll. The Cattell-Horn-Carroll (CHC) hierarchical model of intelligence still has *g* at the top level with fluid and crystallised intelligence at the second level. But alongside them at the second level, there are additional factors such as mental speed, visual and auditory processing, and memory (Carroll, 1993; Cattell, 1967; Horn & Cattell, 1966; Wilhelm & Kyllonen, 2021). At the third level are 80 specialised narrow abilities that explain performance on different tasks. For example, narrow skills for visual processing include abilities such as visual memory and the ability to visualise how complex patterns would look when rotated. It should be noted that this is a dynamic model that has been developed through extensive data collection over many years and is continually being refined (Flanagan & Dixon, 2014; McGrew, 2023).

Online resource 3.1 Cattell–Horn–Carroll hierarchical theory of intelligence

Udacity (2015). Cattell–Horn–Carroll theory. 23 February. Available at: www.youtube.com/watch?v=p2qL72abPfY (Accessed: 28 February 2025)

Application to children in school

Hierarchical models of intelligence have been shown to be useful to educators seeking a more informed understanding of children's cognitive abilities and difficulties experienced in class lessons (see Box 1.1). A positive correlation between cognitive subtests has consistently been found on different IQ scales, showing a commonality of performance across tests and providing evidence of *g* (Jensen & Weng, 1994). A strong correlation was found between Spearman's *g* and educational achievement across different school subjects, with other factors such as motivation, personality, and learning experiences also contributing (Deary et al., 2007; Petrides et al., 2005). Using the CHC model, fluid reasoning and processing speed were found to be strongly related to reading, mathematics achievement, and writing skills in school children (Caemmerer et al., 2018; Cormier et al., 2016; Cormier et al., 2017).

Practitioner educational psychologists may make use of intelligence tests as part of assessment in response to a teacher, parent, or carer expressing concerns about a child's educational progress. While Binet's scales produced a single measure of intelligence, later tests for children commonly used in the UK such as *the Wechsler Intelligence Scale for Children (WISC)* and *British Ability Scales (BAS)* comprise subtests that allow measurement of different domains of children's intelligence, typically including reasoning, verbal comprehension, spatial abilities, memory, and processing speed. WISC-IV and the more recent WISC-V tests both reflect the CHC hierarchical structure (Caemmerer et al., 2018; Reynolds & Keith, 2017), as does BAS (BAS Technical Manual). Children do not perform at exactly the same level on each subtest, so a pattern of each child's strengths and weaknesses is obtained which along with assessment information from other sources can help the educator better understand the nature of the child's difficulties and plan learning activities matching the child's needs.

Intelligence beyond IQ

Both Robert Sternberg and Howard Gardner viewed IQ psychometric testing as too narrow in the type of abilities it tapped.

Triarchic theory of successful intelligence

Robert Sternberg contended that IQ testing omitted abilities that were not scholastic and classroom-based but that were necessary for achievement of successful life outcomes, rather than successful school outcomes. His triarchic theory identified three distinct but interrelated factors (Sternberg, 1985; Sternberg et al., 2001): *creative intelligence* – ability to come up with ideas that are useful in new and unfamiliar situations; *analytical intelligence* –ability to analyse by breaking down a problem into its components and so problem-solve; and *practical intelligence* – ability to adapt your thinking to concrete everyday problems in the real world, using common sense.

Online resource 3.2 Sternberg's successful intelligence
The Brainwaves Video Anthology. (2014). Robert J. Sternberg's successful intelligence. 28 October. Available at: www.youtube.com/watch?v=ow05B4bjGWQ (Accessed: 28 February 2025)

Multiple intelligences theory

Like Sternberg, Howard Gardner also challenged the dominance of psychometrics and argued that while there is extensive statistical evidence built up over the years to support *g* as an important measure, there may also be other useful ways of thinking about intelligence. He proposed that instead of *g*, there are multiple intelligences such as musical, logical–mathematical, spatial, and linguistic abilities that we all possess, with each individual having a different profile of strengths and weaknesses.

Online resource 3.3 Gardner's multiple intelligences theory
TEDxBeaconStreet (2015). Beyond wit and grit: Rethinking the keys to success 10 December. Available at: www.youtube.com/watch?v=IfzrN2yMBaQ (Accessed: 28 February 2025)

Critical thinking task 3.1

How does Gardner's multiple intelligences theory help you better understand your own strengths?
What criticisms might be made of this theory?

Box 3.1 Applying theory to practice for educators: intelligence in the classroom

How can these theories of intelligence help children's learning?

Educators can conclude from these different conceptualisations of intelligence that teachers should arrange a variety of learning opportunities in the classroom in order that children can identify and make the most of their strengths as well as learn how to compensate for their weaknesses. The aim is to match classroom activities to children's intellectual abilities, rather than to their overall level of intellectual ability (IQ). By taking account of the range of possible intelligences identified in these theories, children can demonstrate more achievements than an IQ score alone would predict. In a class of 30 children, it is not feasible to do this individually for each child, but where educators recognise that children learn in different ways, they can arrange to use multiple instructional delivery methods and teaching styles to tap into different strengths. This also allows children who did not understand the material when it was presented one way, to have the opportunity to grasp the ideas when presented another way. Computer-based educational activities are valuable tools for individualised work for this purpose.

For example, instead of the traditional lesson where teacher explains, followed by children carrying out a written exercise with answers to show that they have understood, the teacher presents the lesson in a way that requires careful listening and aural discrimination skills to develop auditory processing abilities; or the teacher designs lessons that make use of visual processing abilities by showing pictures, diagrams, or video. Educators will say that they have been using visual aids for years, but their use here with the goal of building on cognitive processing abilities is underpinned by intelligence theory and supported by research evidence, rather than for the (important) purpose of making the lesson more interesting for better engagement of learners. Increasing speed of processing can be developed by timed problem-solving tasks. Unfamiliar mathematic problems, puzzles, brain teasers, and collaborative problem-solving can be presented to tap fluid intelligence, not only as extension activities. Traditional classroom academic skills such as reading, writing, and mathematics build on crystallised intelligence. Short-term memory skills can be developed by learning songs, poems, and facts, and reproducing patterns from memory. Accommodation in the classroom can be made for children with persistent memory difficulties by providing notes and prompts (Lynch & Warner, 2012; Sternberg et al., 2009).

Sternberg, Torff, and Grigorenko (1998) carried out a study that showed that an educational intervention based on Sternberg's triarchic theory of successful intelligence improved school achievement. They distinguished teaching and assessment for analytic learning that focused on compare and contrast questions for learners to evaluate; creative activities that used imagination and discovery skills; and practical teaching and assessment activities that required learners to apply and make use of their learning. The authors provided examples for a US social studies class: analytic – why is a state governor needed and what are its privileges and limitations? creative – write a story about visiting a place where no one follows rules; and practical – describe what steps you would take to organise an election for class president. The authors emphasise that assessment activities must match the abilities and skills being taught. If teaching covers a range of abilities but assessment just makes use of memory for facts, this gives learners a confused message about what is important.

Cognitive theories

Piaget's stage theory of **cognitive development** was previously outlined in Chapter 1. He identified four developmental stages: sensori-motor, pre-operational, concrete operational, and formal operational. Piaget, like Binet, was interested in the wrong answers that children gave as it allowed him to understand how children's thinking developed. In Chapter 1, we saw that children at the pre-operational stage had difficulty with conservation of quantity. Piaget found that children at this stage of cognitive development had similar difficulties with conservation of length and of number.

Cognitive development Process of change in children as their thinking grows and matures. Change can be gradual or a more abrupt transition from one stage of thinking to the next.

Conservation of number

The problem here is that, in Piaget's studies, children of reception class age thought a spread-out long row of four counters had more counters than a row of four counters arranged in a short row close together. Piaget viewed this as a problem of the child's thinking being dominated by one perceptual dimension and lacking the cognitive flexibility to manipulate that. Piaget concluded that children at this stage did not properly understand the concept of number and that only adding or taking away a counter could change the number to make one row more/less. This finding was replicated by many subsequent researchers. Such a lack of understanding of the meaning of 'four' has serious implications for educators working with children on teaching counting and early number bonds.

Box 3.2 Applying theory to practice for educators: Piaget in the classroom

What does Piaget's research on conservation of number mean for teachers in early years classrooms?

The traditional early 20th-century view of education was that children were empty vessels to be passively filled by adults with knowledge which they 'learned' by rote and that they demonstrated this learning by repetition of the information. Piaget showed us that this was not how learning occurred, and that children's early understanding of a concept is actually very different to that of the adult. Children actively construct knowledge and understanding by interacting with their environment to build schema, blocks of knowledge that relate to each other in a framework. This theory is known as **constructivism.**

Constructivism Children actively try to make meaning from their experiences to build their own understanding of the world.

Children's understanding, their schemas, constantly grow and change. New information is integrated into their understanding through the complementary processes of **assimilation** and **accommodation.** New information that fits into existing schemas is assimilated and absorbed into the current mental framework. New information that initiates a radical rethink of current understandings requires accommodation of existing schema, a major change in the mental framework. For example, understanding that four counters stretched out in a long row are the same number as four counters bunched together will require accommodation, change to existing schemas or even brand-new schemas in a young child who is just learning this new idea and whose current schema equates length and quantity.

Assimilation New information fits with and is absorbed into the existing mental framework.

Accommodation New information initiates a radical rethink of current understandings and requires a major change in the existing mental framework.

Piaget's stage theory is often interpreted as advocating that the teacher does not try to present new ideas that the child is not developmentally 'ready' to understand. But post-Piagetian research studies have shown that even very young children demonstrated understanding of conservation of number if materials were presented, and questions were asked, in particular ways. This indicates a key role for educators in planning and organising learning experiences that can facilitate advanced concept learning.

Educators teaching young children about number need to provide children with the opportunity to engage with concrete objects and explore quantities to discover for themselves the important concept of conservation. The teacher telling or explaining new number concepts to the child is not likely to result in good understanding. The child needs to research the new ideas through physical interaction with objects. The teacher needs to plan and organise suitable materials and activities for this new learning to occur.

Online resource 3.4 Piaget's epistemological concepts
Who the hell is? (2022). Schemas assimilation and accommodation: Jean Piaget's epistemological concepts. 8 October. Available at: www.youtube.com/watch?v=g3JfSIptQqE (Accessed: 28 February 2025)

Critical evaluation of Piaget's stage theory

In Piaget's classic study, the child is shown two rows of counters of the same length, equally spaced. The child is asked: 'Which row has more or are they the same?' to which the child answers that they are the same. One row is then spread out more, and the child is asked the same question a second time. Critics have argued that this interpretation may underestimate children's understanding of number and that because the question is being asked again, the child now may think their first answer was wrong, so they make a different reply. Or the child thinks that because the adult is asking the question again, it now refers to length, not number.

Later research showed that the pre-operational child in certain situations could demonstrate conservation of number. In McGarrigle and Donaldson's (1974) study, the child is told that a naughty teddy, who likes to spoil the game, moves the counters. Using this method of accidental change, rather than the adult making the change, most 4- and 5-year-olds were able to conserve number. McGarrigle and Donaldson's findings suggested that children can be misled by interactional aspects of the setting. In a later study, though, a row of boats floated apart, so neither an adult nor a naughty teddy made the change (Miller, 1982). Children still made the conservation of number error. In yet another study where children were only asked the conservation question once, 5–7-year-olds made fewer errors. It seems that if the tasks are designed differently, or if children have the opportunity to practise, they can answer correctly at an even younger age (Watanabe, 2017). These apparently conflicting findings together suggest that young children may understand more about number conservation than might be concluded from Piaget's original studies but that they can be easily misdirected and make mistakes (Bryant, 1984).

Moreover, the idea of developmental stages has been subject to criticism. Do children really progress through a hierarchy of discrete, discontinuous stages in the stated sequence and at specified ages? Do some children move faster than others through stages? Can some features of an earlier stage still be present when a child begins to demonstrate characteristics of a higher level? (Lourenço, 2016). In addition, it can be argued that a stage theory should not only describe age-related behavioural changes as does Piaget's theory but should also propose explanations as to what caused the changes (Brainerd, 1978).

Although Piaget's stage theory of cognitive development has been subject to some criticism, nonetheless we recognise the significant contribution it has made to stimulating research exploring children's thinking strategies in simple experimental scenarios, and to our understanding of how children actively construct their understanding of the world, rather than act as passive receptacles of knowledge handed down by adults.

Critical thinking task 3.2

Discuss the usefulness of the concept of stages in child development.

Reading[1]

Educators of young children know that reading does not develop naturally like walking and talking but instead requires instruction and practice. They view the teaching of reading to children as one of their most important tasks as it opens the door to infinite opportunities for independently acquiring new knowledge and experiences. As reading is a long-established cultural practice, you'd expect that it would be straightforward to describe psychological theories of teaching reading. You'd be wrong. In the early 2000s, governments in the UK, the USA, and Australia each commissioned reports on reading instruction, all of which favoured a systematic approach to teaching phonics, meaning regular phonics instructional activities embedded within the early years curriculum. Although there has been extensive research on learning to read, there has been a lack of consensus on what is the best approach, emotively expressed as 'reading wars' (Castles et al., 2018). The 'wars' are about which approach to phonics this should be.

One approach is **analytic phonics**, which advocates a whole-word recognition and whole-language approach. With this method, beginning readers employ a look-and-say method to learn whole words by sight and then learn to analyse the sounds and patterns in word families. They build up a reading vocabulary before initial sounds are taught, learning to blend sounds later in the process. The other approach is **synthetic phonics** where, by sounding and blending small part of words (phonemes), the child learns to build up, to synthesise, the whole word. This was the approach recommended by the Rose Report 2006 as policy for UK schools. Research suggests that as long as phonic teaching is systematic, both these phonic methods can be effective (Ehri et al., 2001; Glazzard, 2017; Johnston et al., 2009; Stainthorp, 2020; Wyse & Goswami, 2008).

> **Analytic phonics** Beginning readers first learn whole words by sight and build up a reading vocabulary before they learn sounds.

> **Synthetic phonics** By sounding and blending small part of words (phonemes), the child learns to read the whole word.

Researchers developed computer simulation models to try to explain how skilled readers carry out a reading activity. Such models allow testing out hypotheses with a view to understanding how children might learn to read words in real life.

Connectionist models

There are various versions of this based on a triangle model because of three types of information that the reader has to encode: orthographic (spelling of the word), phonological (sounds), and semantic (meaning). The reader must coordinate how the word looks visually (orthography) with the sounds that make up the word (phonology) as well as ensure that its meaning makes sense (semantics). (Seidenberg, 2007; Seidenberg & McClelland, 1989).

Dual-route models

These models utilise two separate paths where information is processed. One route is the lexical route, where the reader accesses a dictionary of previously seen words stored in the memory. Using the lexical route, familiar words can be processed (read), but not unfamiliar words or made-up non-words such as *lat*. The second route is non-lexical, by which parts of written words are converted to spoken sounds. Through this route, a non-word such as *lat* can be sounded out and read. Regular words can also be sounded and read. The dual-route cascaded model is a version of the dual-route model following many years of research with skilled readers and adults with acquired dyslexia because of brain damage. This model still has lexical and non-lexical pathways, influenced by connectionist models with feedback loops and interactions between the systems (Brysbaert, 2022; Coltheart et al., 2001; Seidenberg et al., 2022).

Critical thinking task 3.3

What reading methods were used to teach you how to read? How effective were these for you?

We return to the topic of reading in Chapter 11 when we examine the impact of psychological theories on policy and practice.

Summary

This chapter outlined theories of intelligence, of cognitive development, and of literacy. These are key theories that help educators understand the individual child's thinking processes and that they apply to the learning activities they plan in school.

But educational psychology is not only about the child as an individual. The importance of the influence of social context is the focus of the next chapter.

Note

1 Reading here refers to word recognition only. Reading comprehension, reading for meaning, is clearly a key component of developing reading skills, but in this chapter the focus is word recognition.

References/Further reading

Brainerd, C. J. (1978). The stage question in cognitive-developmental theory. *Behavioral and Brain Sciences*, *1*(2), 173–182.

Bryant, P. E. (1984). Piaget, teachers and psychologists. *Oxford Review of Education*, *10*(3), 251–259. https://doi.org/10.1080/0305498840100302

Brysbaert, M. (2022). Word recognition II: Phonological coding in reading. In M. Snowling, C. Hulme, & K. Nation (Eds.), *The science of reading: A handbook* (pp. 79–101). John Wiley.

Caemmerer, J. M., Maddocks, D. L. S., Keith, T. Z., & Reynolds, M. R. (2018). Effects of cognitive abilities on child and youth academic achievement: Evidence from the WISC-V and WIAT-III. *Intelligence*, *68*, 6–20. https://doi.org/10.1016/j.intell.2018.02.005

Carroll, J. B. (1993). *Human cognitive abilities: A survey of factor-analytic studies*. Cambridge University Press.

Castles, A., Rastle, K., & Nation, K. (2018). Ending the reading wars: Reading acquisition from novice to expert. *Psychological Science in the Public Interest*, *19*(1), 5–51 (Psychological science in the public interest).

Cattell, R. B. (1943). The measurement of adult intelligence. *Psychological Bulletin*, *40*(3), 153–193. https://doi.org/10.1037/h0059973

Cattell, R. B. (1967). The theory of fluid and crystallized general intelligence checked at the 5–6 year-old level. *British Journal of Educational Psychology*, *37*(2), 209–224. https://doi.org/10.1111/j.2044–8279.1967.tb01930.x

Coltheart, M., Rastle, K., Perry, C., Langdon, R., & Ziegler, J. (2001). DRC: A dual route cascaded model of visual word recognition and reading aloud. *Psychological Review*, *108*(1), 204.

Cormier, D. C., Bulut, O., McGrew, K. S., & Frison, J. (2016). The role of Cattell–Horn–Carroll (CHC) cognitive abilities in predicting writing achievement during the school-age years. *Psychology in the Schools*, *53*(8), 787–803. https://doi.org/10.1002/pits.21945

Cormier, D. C., Bulut, O., McGrew, K. S., & Singh, D. (2017). Exploring the relations between Cattell–Horn–Carroll (CHC) cognitive abilities and mathematics achievement. *Applied Cognitive Psychology*, *31*(5), 530–538. https://doi.org/10.1002/acp.3350

Deary, I. J., Strand, S., Smith, P., & Fernandes, C. (2007). Intelligence and educational achievement. *Intelligence*, *35*(1), 13–21. https://doi.org/10.1016/j.intell.2006.02.001

Ehri, L. C., Nunes, S. R., Stahl, S. A., & Willows, D. M. (2001). Systematic phonics instruction helps students learn to read: Evidence from the National Reading Panel's meta-analysis. *Review of Educational Research*, *71*(3), 393–447.

Flanagan, D. P., & Dixon, S. G. (2014). The Cattell-Horn-Carroll theory of cognitive abilities. In C. R. Reynolds, K. J. Vannest, & E. Fletcher-Janzen (Eds.), *Encyclopedia of Special Education*. Wiley. https://doi.org/10.1002/9781118660584.ese0431

Glazzard, J. (2017). Assessing reading development through systematic synthetic phonics. *English in Education*, *51*(1), 44–57.

Horn, J. L., & Cattell, R. B. (1966). Refinement and test of the theory of fluid and crystallized general intelligences. *Journal of Educational Psychology*, *57*(5), 253.

Hunt, E. (1983). On the nature of intelligence. *Science*, *219*(4581), 141–146.

Jensen, A. R., & Weng, L.-J. (1994). What is a good g? *Intelligence*, *18*(3), 231–258. https://doi.org/10.1016/0160-2896(94)90029-9

Johnston, R. S., Watson, J. E., & Logan, S. (2009). Enhancing word reading, spelling and reading comprehension skills with synthetic phonics teaching: Studies in Scotland and England. In In C. Wood & V. Connelly (Eds.), *Contemporary perspectives on reading and spelling* (pp. 233–250). Routledge.

Kovacs, K., & Pléh, C. (2023). William Stern: The relevance of his program of 'differential psychology' for contemporary intelligence measurement and research. *Journal of Intelligence*, *11*(3), 41.

Lourenço, O. M. (2016). Developmental stages, Piagetian stages in particular: A critical review. *New Ideas in Psychology*, *40*, 123–137.

Lynch, S. A., & Warner, L. (2012). A new theoretical perspective of cognitive abilities. *Childhood Education*, *88*(6), 347–353. https://doi.org/10.1080/00094056.2012.741472

McGarrigle, J., & Donaldson, M. (1974). Conservation accidents. *Cognition*, *3*(4), 341–350. https://doi.org/10.1016/0010-0277(74)90003-1

McGrew, K. S. (2023). Carroll's three-stratum (3S) cognitive ability theory at 30 years: Impact, 3S-CHC theory clarification, structural replication, and cognitive–achievement psychometric network analysis extension. *Journal of Intelligence*, *11*(2), 32.

Miller, S. A. (1982). On the generalizability of conservation: A comparison of different kinds of transformation. *British Journal of Psychology*, *73*(2), 221–230.

Petrides, K. V., Chamorro-Premuzic, T., Frederickson, N., & Furnham, A. (2005). Explaining individual differences in scholastic behaviour and achievement. *British Journal of Educational Psychology*, *75*(2), 239–255.

Reynolds, M. R., & Keith, T. Z. (2017). Multi-group and hierarchical confirmatory factor analysis of the Wechsler Intelligence Scale for Children—Fifth Edition: What does it measure? *Intelligence*, *62*, 31–47.

Seidenberg, M. S. (2007). *Connectionist models of reading*. Oxford Handbook of Psycholinguistics.

Seidenberg, M. S., Farry-Thorn, M., & Zevin, J. D. (2022). Models of word reading: What have we learned? In M. H. Snowling, C. & K. Nation (Eds.), *The science of reading: A handbook* (pp. 36–59). John Wiley and Sons.

Seidenberg, M. S., & McClelland, J. L. (1989). A distributed, developmental model of word recognition and naming. *Psychological Review*, *96*(4), 523.

Stainthorp, R. (2020). A national intervention in teaching phonics: A case study from England. *The Educational and Developmental Psychologist*, *37*(2), 114–122.

Sternberg, R. J. (1985). *Beyond IQ: A triarchic theory of human intelligence*. Cambridge University Press.

Sternberg, R. J., Castejón, J., Prieto, M., Hautamäki, J., & Grigorenko, E. L. (2001). Confirmatory factor analysis of the Sternberg Triarchic Abilities Test in three international samples: An empirical test of the triarchic theory of intelligence. *European Journal of Psychological Assessment*, *17*(1), 1.

Sternberg, R. J., Jarvin, L., & Grigorenko, E. L. (2009). *Teaching for wisdom, intelligence, creativity, and success*. Corwin Press.

Sternberg, R. J., Torff, B., & Grigorenko, E. (1998). Teaching for successful intelligence raises school achievement. *The Phi Delta Kappan*, *79*(9), 667–669.

Watanabe, N. (2017). Acquiring Piaget's conservation concept of numbers, lengths, and liquids as ordinary play. *Journal of Educational and Developmental Psychology*, *7*(1), 210–217.

Wilhelm, O., & Kyllonen, P. (2021). To predict the future, consider the past: Revisiting Carroll (1993) as a guide to the future of intelligence research. *Intelligence*, *89*, 101585. https://doi.org/10.1016/j.intell.2021.101585

Wyse, D., & Goswami, U. (2008). Synthetic phonics and the teaching of reading. *British Educational Research Journal*, *34*(6), 691–710.

Chapter 4

Child in social context

This chapter complements our previous consideration of the child's intellectual development at the individual level by addressing key theories that educational psychology uses to study the social context of learning and emotional aspects of behaviour. We examine how social interaction with an educator can support the child's learning, through the theories of Vygotsky, Bruner, and Feuerstein. We will then explore the role of beliefs and judgements in learner motivation and outcomes with Bandura's social–cognitive theory and Weiner's attribution theory. The importance of secure attachment with the primary caregiver for emotional wellbeing in school is discussed through the work of Bowlby and Ainsworth. Finally, the chapter extends its conception of social psychology as applied to educational psychology to encompass the wider context of Bronfenbrenner's social–ecological theory and biopsychosocial influences.

Learning in a social context: scaffolding

This section outlines theories that examine the role of the adult in encouraging the child's cognitive development through social interaction and providing structure to the learning experience.

Vygotsky's zone of proximal development

Alongside Piaget, another giant of psychology whose theories have significantly influenced education, is Lev Vygotsky, a Russian psychologist. Vygotsky's socio-cultural theory was largely unrecognised in his short lifetime but has been enthusiastically taken on

DOI: 10.4324/9781032691541-6

board since. Piaget's **constructivist** approach to the child's development viewed the child as constructing their own understanding of the world through active interaction with the environment. Vygotsky, however, regarded learning to be the result of learner interactions with the social and cultural context of their environment. This is **social constructivism**. More knowledgeable others, such as teachers, adults, or more capable peers, provide a structure within which children learn new ideas, by having them broken down into smaller manageable chunks.

Constructivism Children actively try to make meaning from their experiences to build their own understanding of the world.

Social constructivism Individuals construct their own understanding of the world through interaction with the social and cultural context of their environment.

Like Piaget, Vygotsky was asked to work on a version of Binet's intelligence test for children in his country. In doing this, each realised that intelligence testing was about quality of intelligence rather than quantity (Lourenço, 2012). Vygotsky recognised a difference in testing what children can do independently, their actual development, and what cognitive tasks ahead of their actual development they can achieve success on with help from a more knowledgeable other. The difference in development between what children can do unaided and what they can do with mediation from someone more expert was referred to by Vygotsky as the **zone of proximal development** (Lourenço, 2012; Shayer, 2003). This is the area where teachers carry out their teaching, designing structured activities, and talking with children to help them develop new insights and understandings. Note that

Zone of proximal development Difference between what children can achieve unaided and what they can do with assistance from someone more expert.

the educator here is working within the zone of proximal development to progress the child's actual development by demonstration and by using leading questions, rather than waiting for a child to achieve a particular developmental stage of readiness for a new concept.

Online resource 4.1 Vygotsky's theory of cognitive development
Sprouts (2020). Vygotsky's theory of cognitive development in social relationships. 28 February. Available at: www.youtube.com/watch?v=8I2hrSRbmHE (Accessed: 28 February 2025).

Dynamic assessment

This is an interactive form of assessment with the aim of identifying the child's potential and the interventions that move the child to the next level of the task. The examiner is an active participant in the assessment, guiding and questioning the child towards these new understandings. This instruction is a central part of the assessment process. Compare this with the neutral objective examiner on standardised psychometric tests who must give no clues as to correct responses so that unassisted performance is measured. **Dynamic assessment** understands that assessment of learning depends on both the individual and the context. This method is derived from Vygotskian theory, from criticisms of traditional static psychometric testing and its predictive validity and in particular from acknowledgement of the importance of Vygotsky's zone of proximal development for assessment of learning potential. This form of assessment depends on social interaction to lead the child onwards from the point where traditional assessment measures stop (Dumas et al., 2017; Lidz, 1995).

Dynamic assessment An interactive assessment process that aims to identify the child's potential and which interventions help move the child to the next level of the task.

Reuven Feuerstein was significant in the development of dynamic assessment with his Learning Potential Assessment

Device (LPAD) and his theory of **cognitive modifiability**, the idea that humans are adaptable and that the thinking of any child can be modified with the right support and structuring of new experiences. The initial objection to the LPAD approach was that the instruction that was intended to lead the child through the zone of proximal development was unstandardised. The instructor could be a teacher, a clinician, or at times a parent, so input could be highly varied (Dumas et al., 2020; Tzuriel & Caspi, 2017). In recent years, automated instruction has been used as part of dynamic assessment which allows more standardised, reproducible, and reportable findings (Dumas et al., 2020). Rather than relying on static IQ testing to assess the needs of struggling learners, educators in the USA adopted a *response-to-intervention* approach based on principles of dynamic assessment (Fuchs & Fuchs, 2006; Grigorenko, 2009).

Cognitive modifiability This is the idea that humans are adaptable and that the thinking of any child can be changed with the right support and structuring of new experiences by a more knowledgeable other person, making the child more able to learn.

Online resource 4.2 Feuerstein's dynamic assessment and instrumental enrichment intervention

Sprouts (2021). The Feuerstein method: Learning through mediation. 17 August. Available at: https://sproutsschools.com/feuerstein-method-learning-how-to-learn-through-mediation/ (Accessed: 28 February 2025).

Bruner's scaffolding

Like Piaget, Jerome Bruner was interested in how children move from concrete thinking to abstract. He viewed the learner as active in constructing their own understandings and conceptualised three stages in cognitive growth: the enactive stage, where the baby engages in actions to encode information in memory; iconic, where pictures help the child learn and understand new concepts; and symbolic, where information is encoded using the medium of language symbols, words, numbers, and mathematical relationships (Bruner, 1964).

It was Bruner who first used the term **scaffolding** to describe how an adult tutor can direct the learner to critical features of the task, can model solutions, and can control the parts of the task that are beyond the learner's current competences, so that the learner can succeed on the parts of the task that they are capable of. In this way, the adult structures the learning environment so that the child can achieve more than without this assistance (Wood et al., 1976). Like Vygotsky, Bruner's theoretical approach is social constructivist, focused on the socio-cultural context through which learning occurs.

Scaffolding A teaching style in which an adult structures the learning task and directs the learner to critical features, so encouraging the learner towards greater success than would have been achieved alone.

Box 4.1 Applying theory to practice for educators: social constructivism and scaffolding in the classroom

Ms James is an experienced teacher who understands that children are not empty vessels to be filled passively with knowledge but that they need to engage actively. She also understands that learning is not a solitary activity, but rather it is a social activity. Because of this, she has organised her class into pairs in order that the children can collaborate with a partner on the curricular task she is setting them today. She wants the children to discuss the activity with each other and share their different perspectives.

She recognises that children gain knowledge from their own experience and that the constructivist teacher must structure the environment and provide suitable materials at the right level of difficulty, so that new learning can occur and that she must act as a facilitator or mentor. She expects to ask the children questions, provide prompts, and encourage them to express their ideas (Mugambi, 2018).

Ms James's 5-year-olds are competent working with numbers up to 10, but she wants them now to learn about numbers up to 20. They know the number names to 20 in order. They are familiar with a number line up to 10, but she doesn't want to simply give them a number line to 20. Instead, she wants them to construct it for themselves.

She structures the task by providing the groups with a blank number line with the two ends marked 0 and 20. The puzzle they have to solve is that there are no numbers marked in between. The pairs must decide where they think the numbers, 5, 10, 12, 15, and 18 should be placed on this line.

Ava and Isla finished this task with ease, so Mrs James gave them an incorrect number line she had prepared asking them to spot the order errors. Arjun and Leo were having some difficulty agreeing on how to get started, so Mrs James suggested that they place 5 and 10 first and then prompted them with questions about which of the remaining numbers were more, and which were less, and what this meant about their position on the number line.

Critical thinking task 4.1

What are the similarities and what are the differences in the role of the educator according to Vygotsky, Bruner, and Feuerstein?
Which theory was Ms James applying in Box 4.1 case study?

Social learning theory and social–cognitive theory Bandura

Theories examined in this chapter and the previous one have discussed how children actively try to construct meaning and understanding and how adults can help them do this. Albert Bandura's insightful **social learning theory** stated that we also learn by observation, by watching others and copying what they do (Bandura

Social learning theory Learning by interaction with, and observation of, others and copying what they do.

& Walters, 1977). Parents implicitly understand this when they want their child to be in a class or a group with children who they perceive as more mature, studious, clever, and well-behaved. They intuitively recognise that such children can demonstrate good behaviours that they want their child to imitate. This is known as modelling.

Bandura then further developed social learning theory into **social–cognitive theory** by including cognitive processes such as beliefs and judgements. Behaviourist theory as proposed by John Watson in the early 20th century advocated that if the environment provided the correct training (by conditioning through reinforcement and punishment), child behaviour could be modified and adapted to achieve any desired learning outcome. Bandura's social–cognitive theory, developed 60 years later, also focuses on the role of environmental experiences in shaping learning, but incorporates social learning by observation and in addition emphasises that our thoughts and beliefs also influence our behaviours.

Social cognitive theory Development of social learning theory that also includes cognitive processes such as beliefs, interpretations, and judgements.

Two key interdependent mechanisms of self-directedness within social–cognitive theory are **self-efficacy** and **self-regulation**, the 'dynamic duo' in school performance (Gaskill & Woolfolk Hoy, 2002). Self-efficacy, belief about one's abilities, is a future-oriented belief, a confidence in one's ability to achieve a particular behavioural outcome that generates motivation (Bandura, 1997). Self-regulated learning is the monitoring and evaluation of your beliefs and your performance

Self-efficacy Belief in one's capability to achieve a particular behavioural outcome or result.

Self-regulation Monitoring your beliefs and performance and using this to influence and control future actions, future learning, and goal setting.

and using these cognitions to influence and control future actions, future learning, and goal setting (Bandura, 1991). These concepts encourage reflection and planning and are central to motivation.

Online resource 4.3 Bandura's social–cognitive theory
Dr Yu-Ling Lee (2021). Albert Bandura social-cognitive theory. 17 August. Available at: www.youtube.com/watch?v=mRW45c4_HUI (Accessed: 28 February 2025).

Children's beliefs about their self-efficacy as learners affect self-regulation and are central to successful learning outcomes (Bandura, 1991). School is the main place where children experience social validation of their intellectual competences through teacher feedback on their work and through social comparison of peers in the classroom, in the playground, and on social media groups. Children who have the same cognitive skills will demonstrate different levels of academic achievement depending on how they perceive their own self-efficacy. Efficacy beliefs are therefore influential mediators of academic attainment.

Previous experiences influence efficacy beliefs and social–cognitive theory views **mastery learning** as the most important source of evidence of self-efficacy to an individual. Mastery is where success is achieved on a task, and this makes individuals feel that they have what it takes to succeed on a future task (Bandura, 1977; Bandura, 1997). The teacher's role then is to plan activities to ensure learners can experience success in order to build feelings of self-efficacy and a positive attitude to future learning.

Mastery learning This is where success is achieved on a task making individuals feel that they have what it takes to succeed on a future task.

Online resource 4.4 Mastery learning
TED (2016). Let's teach for mastery – not test scores. 26 September. Available at: www.youtube.com/watch?v=-MTRxRO5SRA (Accessed: 28 February 2025).

The above section emphasises the role of self-efficacy for the learner, but there is an extensive body of research also on teacher self-efficacy. How effective educators perceive different activities they have planned and how effective they believe their work with different groups of learners influence their beliefs that they can have an effect on pupils' future learning and so affect their management, instructional planning, and their teaching practices (Woolfolk et al., 1990; Wray et al., 2022). Research has also focused on antecedents of teacher self-efficacy in order that teachers feel more competent (Tschannen-Moran & Hoy, 2007; Wilson et al., 2020).

Critical thinking task 4.2

You might like to explore your own feelings of self-efficacy in your studies. Go online and search for an educational self-efficacy scale or academic self-efficacy scale.
Reflect on what you learn about your own feelings of self-efficacy and how you might take your findings forward.

> **Communities of practice** Groups who are concerned about the same issues come together to help each learn.

A further development from Bandura's work is that of building **communities of practice**. This approach recognises the importance of social learning within organisations. Groups who share the same concerns or sets of problems, and want to learn new knowledge and competences, come together in a joint enterprise to share insights, advise, and help each other in problem-solving on an ongoing basis (Wenger, 1999; Wenger et al., 2002). Teachers are applying this process to their own learning (Pharo et al., 2014; Sim, 2006). In addition, education researchers have used the theory of communities of practice to study topics that include teacher professional development, inclusive education, and mathematics education (Farnsworth et al., 2016).

Online resource 4.5 Communities of practice website
Creating communities of practice www.communityofpractice.ca/background/what-is-a-community-of-practice/
(Accessed: 28 February 2025).

Beliefs: attribution theory

Bandura's theory recognised the importance of beliefs in children's academic achievements, in particular self-efficacy beliefs. Bernard Weiner also focused on beliefs, but in his case it was attributional beliefs. **Attribution theory** states that one of the ways a person makes sense of a person's behaviour, or their own, or an event, is by attributing the causes of that behaviour or event. In other words, trying to explain the outcome by asking yourself why did this happen, what caused it? So if you do well on an exam, you might attribute your excellent performance to your *ability*, your *effort*, the *ease of the exam*, or that your success is just down to *luck* (Weiner, 1976). Which of the attributions you use to explain the cause of your success will influence your motivation and the success or failure of future achievement outcomes. If you believe the cause to be luck, you will not be motivated to work hard to prepare for your next exam. Note that two of these causes, ability and effort, are internal to the person, and two, exam difficulty and luck, are external. We have here then four causes, ability, effort, task difficulty, and luck, and two dimensions, *internal* and *external*. Although this formulation of influences on behavioural outcomes is deceptively simple, Weiner took 3 years to reach this point in his theory (Weiner, 2010).

> **Attribution** Explanation of what caused an outcome and why it happened.

He subsequently developed these ideas by applying further thought to how this affected student motivation. The two dimensions, internal and external, describe the *locus* of the cause of the behavioural outcome. To further refine his theory, Weiner added two more causal attributions, *stability* and *controllability*, to locus. If you fail your test and attribute that to lack of effort (internal), is that cause stable or could it change? If you attribute it to a harsh marking (external) that might be stable this year when the same teacher is marking your work but not next year when it's a different teacher. If you attribute your failure to your poor ability (internal), then you are likely to view that as stable. If you attribute failure to a stable, unchanging cause, you have little expectation of a better result next time. The third causal dimension alongside locus and stability is controllability. If the cause of your failure on the test was your lack of effort, you can control that by changing the amount of effort you put in next time.

Online resource 4.6 Attribution theory
Denzel Macaraig (2014). Attribution theory of Bernard Weiner. 4 September. Available at: www.youtube.com/watch?v=YMxY9s58tso (Accessed: 28 February 2025).

Educational psychology research has applied attribution theory in school settings to a range of different areas. Examples include attributions for academic achievement (Glasgow et al., 1997; Matteucci & Gosling, 2004; Ngunu et al., 2019; Tuss et al., 1995); bullying (Batanova et al., 2014); children's willingness to help another in a learning task (Bennett & Flores, 1998); persistence in children with learning disabilities (Ayres et al., 1990); preschool children's attributions for success and failure (Valdivieso & Román Sánchez, 2020); and computer problems in post-school students (Maymon et al., 2018).

Attribution theory can be applied to teacher attributions as well as to learner attributions as it is important to identify how teachers attribute children's difficulties in learning and therefore the extent to which they have expectations of change and so can plan their instruction accordingly. Examples of this are primary school teachers' attributions for causes of success and failure on a reading test (Brun et al., 2022) and teachers giving attributional feedback to young pupils in mathematics lessons (Foote, 1999).

Our research team at University of Strathclyde carried out studies comparing attributions of teachers in different roles, mainstream class teachers, mainstream learning support, and special education teachers (Brady & Marks Woolfson, 2008; Marks Woolfson & Brady, 2009; Marks Woolfson et al., 2007). We found these groups differed from each other in their expectations of change and controllability of learner outcomes for children with learning difficulties. Results from attributional research with teachers have implications for pre-service and in-service teacher training and staff development in terms of attribution retraining to change attributions (Graham & Taylor, 2022). Parallel research on parent attributions for their children's behaviour also suggests that changing parental behaviour may require changing parental attributions (Jacobs et al., 2014, 2016; Shapiro et al., 2013).

Critical thinking task 4.3

Search your library's database to explore interventions that aim to change attributions with a view to changing behaviours in students, educators, caregivers.
How successful are these? In the short term? In the long term?

Attachment theory

The first social and emotional relationship that infants and young children form is with a primary caregiver whose role is to provide security and comfort to the child. **Attachment theory** explains that the role of this lasting psychological bond is to allow the child to feel trust that they are sufficiently safe to be able to leave the proximity of the caregiver to explore and learn about the environment and sufficiently safe to form connections with others. The work of John Bowlby (Bowlby, 1969) and, later that of his student, Mary Ainsworth (Ainsworth et al., 1971) most significantly influenced our understanding of attachment between child and caregiver. Ainsworth's research made use of the Strange Situation, an observational procedure in which there are several potential challenges to the child's feelings of security: the unfamiliarity of the room, separation from the caregiver, and interaction with an unfamiliar adult. The stages of the Strange Situation each last about three minutes. They are as follows:

> **Attachment** The infant–caregiver bond through which the infant receives comfort and develops trust and feelings of safety and security.

1 Infant and caregiver are alone together in an unfamiliar observation room having been taken there by a researcher who then leaves.
2 Child is free to explore.
3 Unfamiliar adult comes into the room, initially silent, then talking to caregiver, and then approaching the infant.

4 Caregiver leaves the room, and the infant and stranger are alone together.
5 Caregiver returns and the unfamiliar adult leaves, while the caregiver settles the infant.
6 Caregiver leaves the infant alone.
7 Unfamiliar adult returns and interacts with infant.
8 Caregiver returns and stranger leaves. Child reacts to reunion with caregiver.

Ainsworth and her team identified three main types of attachment from this. A fourth was added later by Main and Solomon (1990). These are secure, insecure-avoidant, insecure-resistant, and disorganised.

Securely attached infants played happily when the caregiver was in the room with them and showed distress when the caregiver left the room. Securely attached infants greeted their caregivers positively when they were reunited at the final stage. Most children fall into this category.

Anxious-avoidant infants did not seem to be upset when their caregiver left the room and did not try to approach when the caregiver returned, indeed avoided the caregiver by turning away.

Anxious-resistant infants were distressed at stage 2, seeming uncomfortable in the strange environment and unwilling to explore the toys. They were upset when their caregiver left but ambivalent towards the caregiver at the reunion stage, appearing angry. They rushed to their caregiver to be consoled but then refused to be comforted.

Disorganised-disoriented attachment is the category added by Main and Solomon. A minority of infants seemed to lack any strategy for coping with the separation and reunions of the Strange Situation and demonstrated unpredictable patterns of behaviour with a confused pattern of approach and avoidance of the caregiver.

Online resource 4.7 Strange Situation

Psychology Unlocked (2017). The Strange Situation. Mary Ainsworth 1969. 27 April Available at: www.youtube.com/watch?v=m_6rQk7jlrc (Accessed: 28 February 2025).

Online resource 4.8 Attachment theory
Mister Simplify (2020). Attachment theory and the stages of attachment. 28 November. Available at: www.youtube.com/watch?v=-67zk6MOQLw (Accessed: 28 February 2025).

Critics of the Strange Situation point out that we are inferring judgements about real-life relationships from a laboratory study with middle-class American mothers. They argue that the infant's behaviour might be very different in a more familiar setting such as their home, or with primary caregivers other than mothers, or in different cultures. It is worth noting that Ainsworth first evolved her three attachment categories from a longitudinal study observing mother–child bonding in Uganda, recognising cultural differences when transferring her methodology to the US study (Ainsworth & Salter, 1967). Since the original study, research investigating cultural variations suggests that cultural sensitivity is required in the assumptions and presentation of the Strange Situation procedure itself, as infants in many cultures are used to multiple caregivers, and that a bond between a child and an individual caregiver is not necessary the typical model of child-rearing. Cultures also differ in their goals for children to develop independence and social interactional skills. Research across different cultures though has found that variability is around the proportions of children in each category but that Ainsworth's categories still hold (Keller, 2013).

Why is the relationship between a baby and its caregiver of any importance to educational psychology? It's because the attachment relationship has been found to predict many later outcomes important for later developmental and educational outcomes. These include academic achievement, social competence, emotion regulation, self-reliance, and recognition of emotions (Dindo et al., 2017; Nivison et al., 2025; Sroufe, 2005; Steele et al., 2008; Weinfield et al., 1997).

Box 4.2 Applying theory to practise for educators: attachment theory and nurture groups

Nurture groups were first set up in London in 1970 by Marjorie Boxall, an educational psychologist working in Hackney, London, who recognised that children start school with very different preschool experiences. The groups were a response to children living in this area of social deprivation who exhibited disruptive, aggressive behaviours leading to their being excluded from school at an early age. Boxall was influenced by attachment theory and the idea that these children were engaging in developmentally inappropriate behaviour because of unmet attachment needs.

The aim of the nurture group was to reproduce the experience of a normal childhood within a nurturing family environment, not by trying to reproduce a caregiver–child attachment but instead an educational attachment. The small special class with 6–12 children would provide the vulnerable child with the opportunity to forge bonds with adult staff that they could trust. They would feel secure enough within the group's structure, homely setting, and daily routine to explore and so learn. Nurture groups are also influenced by Bruner's scaffolding and Vygotsky's zone of proximal development with the individual child supported towards new learning by a more competent adult.

The number of nurture groups grew throughout London and more widely through the UK and beyond, largely through anecdotal evidence from teachers who saw the benefits. There was then a drop in popularity with some groups closing, followed by renewed interest in the approach (Bennathan & Boxall, 2013). There were positive published retrospective descriptive reports of progress, but for the first 30 years there was a limited amount of rigorous, systematic research to provide convincing evidence of their effectiveness. To remedy this, Cooper and Whitebread (2007) carried out a national study in UK and found evidence supporting the descriptive reports that children who attended nurture groups showed improvements in their social, emotional, and behavioural functioning. There also seemed to be carryover beyond the nurture group to the wider school for pupils with emotional difficulties in mainstream classes who did not attend the groups, leading to the concept of the nurturing school. A Glasgow study provided evidence of improved academic attainment (MacKay et al., 2010).

Systematic reviews subsequently offered more compelling support. Hughes and Schlösser (2014) examined 11 papers investigating the effectiveness of nurture groups and concluded that there was evidence that the groups improved emotional wellbeing. Bennett (2015) carried out a systematic review of 62 studies and found a consensus of evidence that nurture groups improved social, emotional, and behavioural outcomes for primary aged children and cautiously concluded from the studies available that they have the potential for improving academic outcomes too.

Further research is needed now to identify what are the necessary elements of nurture groups to achieve these positive outcomes. Is it small class size, balance of needs within the group, teacher characteristics, teacher–child relationship, or having two adults working with the group and modelling behaviour? More research is also needed with secondary school nurture groups, as well as more longitudinal research to determine how long any effects last. In conclusion, more high-quality research on this topic is required now.

Critical thinking task 4.4

How convincing is the evidence that nurture groups work?

Wider social context Bronfenbrenner

In this chapter, we have been looking at the child's relationship with the caregiver and also within the social context of the classroom. We can go beyond this though to consider other social contexts in the wider ecology within which the child exists and which influence the child's development. Bronfenbrenner's (1979) **social ecological** model

Social ecological theory This conceptualisation has social microsystems that directly or indirectly influence the child's development nested within each other like a Russian doll. Thus, the family microsystem is nested within the wider family system and that is nested within the local community, and so on to local government, wider society, and culture.

conceptualised a series of nested social systems (think Russian dolls with smaller dolls nested inside larger ones) that influence each other. Those systems that the child participates in are referred to as microsystems, for example, the family **microsystem**, the classroom and school. These microsystems are nested within the wider community which in turn is nested within a wider society. **Mesosystems** are the systems that link the microsystems. The relationship between school and parents, or school and the local community, are examples of mesosystems. **Exosystems** are systems beyond the child like the local council or the government, whose education policies will affect the child's experience in school, but with whom the child has no direct contact.

Microsystem The systems that the child participates directly in are referred to as microsystems, for example, the family and the school.

Mesosystem The systems that link the microsystems. Examples of mesosystems are the relationship linking school and parents or between school and the local community.

Exosystem This is a system such as the district council that the child has no direct contact with but whose policies affect the child's experience in school.

I was significantly influenced by the insights offered by Bronfenbrenner's model and shared these both in training **practitioner educational psychologists** and in writing for professional publications. Over the last 20 years instead of a focus only on assessment of the individual child's difficulties, UK practitioner educational psychologists have also carried out assessment and

Practitioner/professional educational psychologist School psychologist who carries out applied work with children, school staff, carers, and families. This might be at the level of the individual child, the family, the classroom, the school, or the school district.

intervention that take into account the influences of microsystems in which the child lives, plays, and learns and mesosystems such as the relationships between home and school (Marks Woolfson, 2017; Marks Woolfson et al., 2003). This means that the work of the modern educational psychologist increasingly comprises indirect work with key adults in order to effect change in the ecological systems that influence the child's experience (Conoley et al., 2020).

Online resource 4.9 Bronfenbrenner's social ecological theory
Rachelle Tannenbaum (2018). Bronfenbrenner's ecological theory. 3 January. Available at: www.youtube.com/watch?v=HV4E05BnoI8 (Accessed: 28 February 2025).

Biopsychosocial model in educational psychology

Biopsychosocial The influence of a combination of multiple factors, including psychological, social influence and also biological factors such as genetics and physical health.

Extending the idea of a multi-causal model leads us to a **biopsychosocial** approach which recognises that multiple factors from different disciplines influence children's learning, behaviour, and mental health. As well as psychological factors as discussed over the last two chapters and different levels of social influence identified in Bronfenbrenner's social ecological theory, there are also biological factors such as genetics, physical health, and personal characteristics to be considered. Sameroff's unified theory of human development captures this where he views the self as composed of a series of interactions between psychological, social, and biological processes (Sameroff, 2010). Biopsychosocial models are influential in health and clinical psychology where clinicians who traditionally focused on biomedical aspects of health and illness are aware that it is important to take a more holistic, interdisciplinary approach and consider how psychosocial factors might also influence patients' physical and mental wellbeing.

Online resource 4.10 Biopsychosocial model applied to health and illness

Shorts in psychology (2021). The biopsychosocial model. 1 February. Available at: www.youtube.com/watch?v=eN6pCOMewNY (Accessed: 28 February 2025).

Attention to investigating the interplay of biopsychosocial factors can help both professional and academic educational psychologists better understand the sources of individual differences in children's behaviour, academic performance, and health and well-being. Although there is recognition that biopsychosocial models have the potential to make a valuable contribution to the professional educational psychology (Norwich, 2016), they have not yet been used to any significant extent in the field.

The International Classification of Functioning, Disability and Health – Children and Youth (ICF-CY) developed by World Health Organisation is a practical application of this interdisciplinary biopsychosocial thinking (Simeonsson, 2009; Simeonsson et al., 2003), but apart from Portugal and Switzerland, international take-up has been limited (Hollenweger, 2011; Lebeer et al., 2011; Sanches-Ferreira et al., 2014). This is perhaps due to the time-consuming nature of its inter-professional information collection and also the ICF-CY's medical diagnostic focus, which may not provide sufficient information to aid intervention planning for educational psychology professionals (Norwich, 2016).

Research in educational psychology seems currently to make greater use of biopsychosocial models than do practitioners in schools. For example, a recent study to examine how personality dimensions influence student engagement and participation in school made use of a biopsychosocial model (Moreira et al., 2021). Kranzler et al. (2020) explain how research on bullying can make use of biopsychosocial insights and recommended that what we need to do now is to translate the outcomes of biopsychosocial research into effective educational interventions. As practitioner psychologists cannot be experts in all the areas encompassed in a biopsychosocial model, interdisciplinary collaboration with other professionals is required.

Critical thinking task 4.5

How could educators make use of a biopsychosocial model in their classroom practice?

Box 4.3 Biopsychosocial theory applied to research on bullying in schools

Kranzler et al. (2020) provide an example of how a biopsychosocial ecological approach can provide insight into bullying, a complex problematic behaviour in schools with a view to helping us better understand how to design interventions, both preventive and reactive. The paper begins its biopsychosocial analysis by reviewing bullying research at the individual level. For example, biological factors at individual level include sex, with males more likely to be both bullies and victims. Psychological and social factors at individual level include social skills, attitudes, as well as the child's individual perceptions and beliefs.

Next the authors identify bullying research focused on microsystems, such as school climate, school bullying prevention policies, families, and local neighbourhood and interactions (mesosystems) between these microsystems. The broader exosystem environments have also been studied in bullying research such as the legal system and school boards. The child does not interact with these systems directly, but their policies around bullying affect the child as lower rates of bullying have been reported where there are anti-bullying policies.

Finally, Kranzler et al. consider the macrosystem with respect to bullying as the influence of society's cultural norms, including the social stigmas and biases attached to some characteristics or identities that make young people feel devalued. Young people therefore may experience bullying because they are disabled or because of their religious beliefs or their ethnicity. Application of a biopsychosocial model has a valuable contribution to make to practitioner educational psychologists' understanding of the experience of minority groups with respect to wider systemic issues of equity and diversity in schools (Bartolo, 2010).

Summary

This chapter outlined theories used in educational psychology that examine the child's learning and behaviour within a social context, starting with the influence of social interaction with the caregiver and the educator and extending to wider socio-cultural and biological influences.

An important area in educational psychology that also makes use of social psychological understandings is that of bullying and violence in schools. These theories are the topic of the next chapter.

References/Further reading

Ainsworth, M., Bell, S., & Stayton, D. (1971). Individual differences in Strange Situation behavior of one year olds. In H. Schaffer (Ed.), *The origins of human social relations* (pp. 17–58). Academic Press.

Ainsworth, M., & Salter, D. (1967). *Infancy in Uganda. Infant care and the growth of love*. Johns Hopkins University Press.

Ayres, R., Cooley, E., & Dunn, C. (1990). Self-concept, attribution, and persistence in learning-disabled students. *Journal of School Psychology*, *28*(2), 153–163. https://doi.org/10.1016/0022-4405(90)90006-S

Bandura, A. (1977). Self-efficacy: Toward a unifying theory of behavioral change. *Psychological Review*, *84*(2), 191–215.

Bandura, A. (1991). Social cognitive theory of self-regulation. *Organizational Behavior and Human Decision Processes*, *50*(2), 248–287. https://doi.org/10.1016/0749-5978(91)90022-L

Bandura, A. (1997). *Self efficacy: The exercise of control*. W.H. Freeman and Co.

Bandura, A., & Walters, R. H. (1977). *Social learning theory* (Vol. 1). Prentice Hall.

Bartolo, P. A. (2010). Why school psychology for diversity? *School Psychology International*, *31*(6), 567–580.

Batanova, M., Espelage, D. L., & Rao, M. A. (2014). Early adolescents' willingness to intervene: What roles do attributions, affect, coping, and self-reported victimization play? *Journal of School Psychology*, *52*(3), 279–293. https://doi.org/10.1016/j.jsp.2014.02.001

Bennathan, M., & Boxall, M. (2013). *Effective intervention in primary schools: Nurture groups* (2nd ed.). David Fulton Publishers.

Bennett, H. (2015). Results of the systematic review on nurture groups' effectiveness. *The International Journal of Nurture in Education*, *1*(1), 3–7.

Bennett, T. R., & Flores, M. S. (1998). Help giving in achievement contexts: A developmental and cultural analysis of the effects of children's attributions and affects on their willingness to help. *Journal of Educational Psychology, 90*(4), 659–669.

Bowlby, J. (1969). *Attachment and loss.* Random House.

Brady, K., & Marks Woolfson, L. (2008). What teacher factors influence their attributions for children's difficulties in learning? *British Journal of Educational Psychology, 78*, 527–544.

Bronfenbrenner, U. (1979). *The ecology of human development: Experiments by nature and design.* Harvard University Press.

Brun, L., Dompnier, B., & Pansu, P. (2022). A latent profile analysis of teachers' causal attribution for academic success or failure. *European Journal of Psychology of Education, 37*(1), 185–206.

Bruner, J. S. (1964). The course of cognitive growth. *American Psychologist, 19*(1), 1.

Conoley, J. C., Powers, K., & Gutkin, T. B. (2020). How is school psychology doing: Why hasn't school psychology realized its promise? *School Psychology, 35*(6), 367–374.

Cooper, P., & Whitebread, D. (2007). The effectiveness of nurture groups on student progress: evidence from a national research study. *Emotional and Behavioural Difficulties, 12*(3), 171–190. https://doi.org/10.1080/13632750701489915

Dindo, L., Brock, R. L., Aksan, N., Gamez, W., Kochanska, G., & Clark, L. A. (2017). Attachment and effortful control in toddlerhood predict academic achievement over a decade later. *Psychological Science, 28*(12), 1786–1795.

Dumas, D., McNeish, D., & Greene, J. A. (2020). Dynamic measurement: A theoretical–psychometric paradigm for modern educational psychology. *Educational Psychologist, 55*(2), 88–105.

Dumas, D. G., McNeish, D. M., & Greene, J. A. (2017). Dynamic measurement modeling: Using nonlinear growth models to estimate student learning capacity. *Educational Researcher, 46*(6), 284–292.

Farnsworth, V., Kleanthous, I., & Wenger-Trayner, E. (2016). Communities of practice as a social theory of learning: A conversation with Etienne Wenger. *British Journal of Educational Studies, 64*(2), 139–160.

Foote, C. J. (1999). Attribution feedback in the elementary classroom. *Journal of Research in Childhood Education, 13*(2), 155–166.

Fuchs, D., & Fuchs, L. S. (2006). Introduction to response to intervention: What, why, and how valid is it? *Reading Research Quarterly, 41*(1), 93–99.

Gaskill, P. J., & Woolfolk Hoy, A. (2002). Self-efficacy and self-regulated learning: The dynamic duo in school performance. In J. Aronson (Ed.), *Improving academic achievement* (pp. 185–208). Academic Press. https://doi.org/10.1016/B978-012064455-1/50012-9

Glasgow, K. L., Dornbusch, S. M., Troyer, L., Steinberg, L., & Ritter, P. L. (1997). Parenting styles, adolescents' attributions, and educational outcomes in nine heterogeneous high schools. *Child Development*, *68*(3), 507–529.

Graham, S., & Taylor, A. Z. (2022). The power of asking why?: Attribution retraining programs for the classroom teacher. *Theory into Practice*, *61*(1), 5–22.

Grigorenko, E. L. (2009). Dynamic assessment and response to intervention: Two sides of one coin. *Journal of Learning Disabilities*, *42*(2), 111–132.

Hollenweger, J. (2011). Development of an ICF-based eligibility procedure for education in Switzerland. BMC public health,

Hughes, N. K., & Schlösser, A. (2014). The effectiveness of nurture groups: A systematic review. *Emotional and Behavioural Difficulties*, *19*(4), 386–409.

Jacobs, M., Marks Woolfson, L., & Hunter, S. (2014). Parental causal attributions for child misbehaviour and their relationship with parenting strategies: A comparison between parents of children with IDD and typically developing children. *Journal of Applied Research in Intellectual Disabilities*, *27*(4), 360–360.

Jacobs, M., Marks Woolfson, L., & Hunter, S. (2016). Attributions of stability, control and responsibility: How parents of children with intellectual disabilities view their child's problematic behaviour and its causes. *Journal of Applied Research in Intellectual Disabilities*, *29*, 58–70.

Keller, H. (2013). Attachment and culture. *Journal of Cross-Cultural Psychology*, *44*(2), 175–194.

Kranzler, J. H., Floyd, R. G., Bray, M. A., & Demaray, M. K. (2020). Past, present, and future of research in school psychology: The biopsychosocial ecological model as an overarching framework. *School Psychology*, *35*(6), 419–427.

Lebeer, J., Birta-Székely, N., Demeter, K., Bohács, K., Candeias, A. A., Sønnesyn, G. ... Dawson, L. (2011). Re-assessing the current assessment practice of children with special education needs in Europe. *School Psychology International*, *33*(1), 69–92. https://doi.org/10.1177/0143034311409975

Lidz, C. S. (1995). Dynamic assessment and the legacy of L.S. Vygotsky. *School Psychology International*, *16*(2), 143–153. https://doi.org/10.1177/0143034395162005

Lourenço, O. (2012). Piaget and Vygotsky: Many resemblances, and a crucial difference. *New Ideas in Psychology*, *30*(3), 281–295.

MacKay, T., Reynolds, S., & Kearney, M. (2010). From attachment to attainment: The impact of nurture groups on academic achievement. *Educational and Child Psychology*, *27*(3), 100.

Main, M., & Solomon, J. (1990). Procedures for identifying infants as disorganized/disoriented during the Ainsworth Strange Situation. In *Attachment in the preschool years: Theory, research, and intervention* (pp. 121–160). The University of Chicago Press.

Marks Woolfson, L. (2017). The Woolfson et al Integrated Framework: An executive framework for service-wide delivery. In B. Kelly, L. M. Woolfson, & J. Boyle (Eds.), *Frameworks for practice in educational psychology* (2nd ed., pp. 151–166). Jessica Kingsley Publishers.

Marks Woolfson, L., & Brady, K. (2009). An investigation of factors impacting on mainstream teachers' beliefs about teaching students with learning difficulties. *Educational Psychology*, *29*(2), 221–238.

Marks Woolfson, L., Grant, E., & Campbell, L. (2007). A comparison of special, general and support teachers' controllability and stability attributions for children's difficulties in learning. *Educational Psychology*, *27*(2), 295–306.

Marks Woolfson, L., Whaling, R., Stewart, A., & Monsen, J. (2003). An integrated framework to guide educational psychologist practice. *Educational Psychology in Practice*, *19*, 283–302.

Matteucci, M. C., & Gosling, P. (2004). Italian and French teachers faced with pupil's academic failure: The "norm of effort". *European Journal of Psychology of Education*, *19*, 147–166.

Maymon, R., Hall, N., Thomas, G., Chiarella, A., & Rahimi, S. (2018). Technology, attribution, and emotions in post-secondary education: An applications of Weiner's attribution theory to academic computing problems. *PLoS One*, *13(3)*. https://doi.org/10.1371/journal.pone.0103443

Moreira, P. A., Inman, R. A., Cloninger, K., & Cloninger, C. R. (2021). Student engagement with school and personality: A biopsychosocial and person-centred approach. *British Journal of Educational Psychology*, *91*(2), 691–713.

Mugambi, M. M. (2018). Linking constructivism theory to classroom practice. *International Journal of Humanities Social Sciences and Education*, *5*(9), 96–104.

Ngunu, S., Kinai, T., Ndambuki, P., & Mwaura, P. (2019). Causal attributions as correlates of secondary school students' academic achievement. *Education Research International*, *2019*, 1–7.

Nivison, M., Caldo, P. D., Magro, S. W., Raby, K. L., Groh, A. M., Vandell, D. L. ... Roisman, G. I. (2025). The predictive validity of the strange situation procedure: Evidence from registered analyses of two landmark longitudinal studies. *Development and Psychopathology. First* view, *37*(1), 147–163. https://doi.org/10.1017/S0954579423001487

Norwich, B. (2016). Conceptualizing special educational needs using a biopsychosocial model in England: The prospects and challenges of using the international classification of functioning framework. *Frontiers in Education*, *1*, 5.

Pharo, E., Davison, A., McGregor, H., Warr, K., & Brown, P. (2014). Using communities of practice to enhance interdisciplinary teaching: Lessons from four Australian institutions. *Higher Education Research & Development*, *33*(2), 341–354.

Sameroff, A. (2010). A unified theory of development: A dialectic integration of nature and nurture. *Child Development*, *81*(1), 6–22.

Sanches-Ferreira, M., Silveira-Maia, M., & Alves, S. (2014). The use of the International Classification of Functioning, Disability and Health, version for Children and Youth (ICF-CY), in Portuguese special education assessment and eligibility procedures: the professionals' perceptions. *European Journal of Special Needs Education*, *29*(3), 327–343. https://doi.org/10.1080/08856257.2014.908025

Shapiro, M., Kazemi, E., & Weiner, B. (2013). Whose fault is it anyway: How do parents respond to their child's setbacks? *Social Psychology of Education*, *16*, 95–109.

Shayer, M. (2003). Not just Piaget; not just Vygotsky, and certainly not Vygotsky as alternative to Piaget. *Learning and Instruction*, *13*(5), 465–485. https://doi.org/10.1016/S0959-4752(03)00092-6

Sim, C. (2006). Preparing for professional experiences—incorporating pre-service teachers as 'communities of practice'. *Teaching and Teacher Education*, *22*(1), 77–83.

Simeonsson, R. J. (2009). ICF-CY: A universal tool for documentation of disability. *Journal of Policy and Practice in Intellectual Disabilities*, *6*(2), 70–72. https://doi.org/10.1111/j.1741-1130.2009.00215.x

Simeonsson, R. J., Leonardi, M., Lollar, D., Bjorck-Akesson, E., Hollenweger, J., & Martinuzzi, A. (2003). Applying the International Classification of Functioning, Disability and Health (ICF) to measure childhood disability. *Disability and Rehabilitation*, *25*(11–12), 602–610. https://doi.org/10.1080/0963828031000137117

Sroufe, L. A. (2005). Attachment and development: A prospective, longitudinal study from birth to adulthood. *Attachment & Human Development*, *7*(4), 349–367.

Steele, H., Steele, M., & Croft, C. (2008). Early attachment predicts emotion recognition at 6 and 11 years old. *Attachment & Human Development*, *10*(4), 379–393.

Tschannen-Moran, M., & Hoy, A. W. (2007). The differential antecedents of self-efficacy beliefs of novice and experienced teachers. *Teaching and Teacher Education*, *23*(6), 944–956.

Tuss, P., Zimmer, J., & Ho, H. (1995). Causal attributions of underachieving fourth-grade students in China, Japan, and the United States. *Journal of Cross-Cultural Psychology*, *26*(4), 408–425.

Tzuriel, D., & Caspi, R. (2017). Intervention for peer mediation and mother-child interaction: The effects on children's mediated learning strategies and cognitive modifiability. *Contemporary Educational Psychology*, *49*, 302–323.

Valdivieso, L. L., & Román Sánchez, J. M. (2020). Causal attributions in early childhood education: A new categorization system. *Psicothema*, *32(3)*, 366–373.

Weiner, B. (1976). An attributional approach for educational psychology. *Review of Research in Education*, *4*(1), 179–209.

Weiner, B. (2010). The development of an attribution-based theory of motivation: A history of ideas. *Educational Psychologist*, *45*(1), 28–36. https://doi.org/10.1080/00461520903433596

Weinfield, N. S., Ogawa, J. R., & Sroufe, L. A. (1997). Early attachment as a pathway to adolescent peer competence. *Journal of Research on Adolescence*, *7*(3), 241–265. https://doi.org/10.1207/s15327795jra0703_1

Wenger, E. (1999). *Communities of practice: Learning, meaning, and identity*. Cambridge University Press.

Wenger, E., McDermott, R., & Snyder, W. (2002). *Cultivating communities of practice: A guide to managing knowledge*. Harvard Business School Press.

Wilson, C., Marks Woolfson, L., & Durkin, K. (2020). School environment and mastery experience as predictors of teachers' self-efficacy beliefs towards inclusive teaching. *International Journal of Inclusive Education*, *24*, 218–234. https://doi.org/10.1080/13603116.2018.1455901

Wood, D., Bruner, J. S., & Ross, G. (1976). The role of tutoring in problem solving. *Journal of Child Psychology and Psychiatry*, *17*(2), 89–100.

Woolfolk, A. E., Rosoff, B., & Hoy, W. K. (1990). Teachers' sense of efficacy and their beliefs about managing students. *Teaching and Teacher Education*, *6*(2), 137–148. https://doi.org/10.1016/0742-051X(90)90031-Y

Wray, E., Sharma, U., & Subban, P. (2022). Factors influencing teacher self-efficacy for inclusive education: A systematic literature review. *Teaching and Teacher Education*, *117*, 103800. https://doi.org/10.1016/j.tate.2022.103800

Chapter 5

More about the child in social context: Bullying in schools

This chapter is an extension of the previous chapter in that it also discusses social theories in educational psychology. In this chapter though, these theories are all applied to explain the phenomenon of bullying in schools. Sadly, everyone has some understanding of what bullying is from their own schooldays and is probably readily able to recall specific examples. We regularly read in the press about present-day examples, often with desperate outcomes for the victim. Educational psychology researchers and practitioners have applied their efforts to develop theoretical approaches to gain better understanding of bullying in schools, in order that schools can carry out anti-bullying interventions. Let's first clarify what is meant by bullying and cyberbullying, and then, we can examine some psychosocial theories that are applied to this topic.

Definition and prevalence

So what exactly is **bullying**? It is repeated aggressive behaviour towards one or more individuals in which there is an imbalance of power (Smith, 2016a). A single incident of aggressive behaviour is not therefore in itself bullying until it becomes a pattern. The behaviour is a systematic abuse of power, where victims are not able to resolve the situation themselves (Smith & Sharp, 2002). Bullying can be direct, such as kicking, pushing, hitting, verbal insults, and name-calling, or it

Bullying Repeated threatening or aggressive behaviour towards one or more individuals in which there is an imbalance of power. This can be direct or indirect.

DOI: 10.4324/9781032691541-7

Box 5.1 Bullying in film and books

As we can see from classic literature, bullying has been around for a long time. The book *Tom Brown's Schooldays* was published in 1857, set in Rugby School, and one of the book's key themes was the bullying of Tom by an older boy, Harry Flashman. Lord of the Flies (1954) explores how bullying emerges when a group of boys are left to their own devices on an island. *To Kill a Mockingbird* (1960) and *Carrie* (1974) both also deal with this theme, as do *Dear Evan Hansen* (2021), *Wicked* (2024), and *Mean Girls* (2024). Academic study of bullying, however, started in 1970 with Dan Olweus's pioneering research on bullying and aggression in 900 Swedish boys. Olweus's subsequent work studying and campaigning against bullying until his death in 2020 has shaped awareness and understanding of bullying internationally and influenced anti-bullying intervention programmes and policies in schools. The Olweus Bullying Prevention Programme (OBPP) will be discussed in Chapter 10.

can be indirect such as the spreading of rumours and excluding the victim from social groups. In direct bullying, the victim knows who the bully is, but may not know in indirect bullying (Rivers & Smith, 1994).

Cyberbullying Carrying out verbally threatening or harassing behaviour using digital means, such as text messages, email, and social media sites. This may be viewed as a form of indirect bullying.

Cyberbullying is a modern variation by which the availability and ubiquity of social networking sites has allowed bullying to extend beyond the school day to the home life of the victim. Some studies view cyberbullying as a form of indirect bullying using digital means as the bully can be anonymous and bullying can be repeated, not by the instigating bully, but by others forwarding the messages or images (Del Rey et al., 2022).

Online resource 5.1 Cyberbullying

Trinity College Dublin. (2017). *Bullying and cyberbullying: Prevalence, psychological impacts, and intervention strategies.* 7 February. Available at: www.youtube.com/watch?v=vTMKYtOJywY (Accessed: 28 February 2025).

UK House of Commons Library reported in 2020 that 29% secondary school head teachers had received reports of physical and non-physical bullying. 14% students or parent/guardians had reported incidents of hurtful remarks on social media. These figures were higher than the European average. Although bullying is a worldwide phenomenon, data on prevalence vary across studies depending on measurement tool used, age of respondents, and how bullying was defined which may differ across studies (Jetelina et al., 2019). Gender differences have been consistently reported with boys more likely to be engaged in aggressive, physical, and direct bullying than girls, who in contrast are more involved in cyberbullying (Smith, 2023). Identity-, or prejudice-based bullying is also a recognised issue, with bullying of minority groups based on gender, sexual orientation, disability, ethnicity, and race (Earnshaw et al., 2018; Gönültaş & Mulvey, 2021).

Online resource 5.2 National bullying helpline

Information and advice for parents, teachers, and students dealing with bullying www.nationalbullyinghelpline.co.uk (Accessed: 28 February 2025).

Let's look now at how educational psychology has studied this serious problem.

Social learning and social cognitive theory

In Chapter 4, we discussed Bandura's social learning and social cognitive theories with respect to educational activities in the classroom. In this chapter, social learning, modelling, observation, and consequences are discussed in relation

Social learning Learning by interaction with, and observation of, others and copying what they do.

to bullying behaviour. Some researchers noted that bullying typically involves an audience of peers observing, or being aware of, the bullying act. It may be that peers witnessing are thus effectively condoning the bullying behaviour, which then acts as a reinforcer of that behaviour. In addition, if the bully is modelling bullying behaviour without sanction, this increases the possibility that peers will be motivated to imitate it (Pepler et al., 2009). Bandura (1973) applied social learning theory and later social cognitive theory to explain aggressive behaviour and how children learn to bully. Added in to social learning theory are cognitions and attitudes regarding whether bullying is acceptable and beliefs about consequences which, along with observation, make it more likely that children learn to bully (Swearer et al., 2014). Social cognitive theory views school bullying behaviour as the outcome of reciprocal triadic interaction between environmental factors such as the peer group and personal beliefs, that is, a triad comprising behaviour, internal beliefs, and social environment (Bussey, 2023; Swearer et al., 2014).

Social cognitive theory Development of social learning theory that also includes cognitive processes such as beliefs, interpretations, and judgements.

Participant role theory

Participant role theory addresses not only bully and victim roles but also the roles of the others in supporting bullying behaviour. Following Olweus' seminal early work on bullying, Salmivalli et al. (1996) took forward our theoretical understanding by studying all of the participant roles in a sample of 573 12–13-year-olds in Finland. They investigated six roles: bully (Sutton et al., 1999), victim, reinforcer (laughs or encourages), assistant

Participant role theory Recognition that in addition to bully and victim, there are other roles in bullying: reinforcer (laughs or encourages), assistant (joins in), defender of victim (helps victim), and bystander (aware of bullying but ignores it).

(joins in), defender of victim (helps victim), and bystander (aware of bullying but ignores it) (Smith, 2016a). The research team related these roles to sociometric status: popular, rejected, neglected, controversial, and average. Their findings suggested that 87% children in a class have a participant role in bullying, with bystander, reinforcer, and defender the most common participant roles. Boys had more active roles in bullying, mostly as reinforcers and assistants. Defenders had the highest social status. Victims, both male and female, had the lowest social status, identified as 'rejected' on the sociometric questionnaire, where participants had to nominate classmates whom they liked most and least (Salmivalli et al., 1996). This social rejection of victims may be both a cause and an outcome of bullying. Olweus (1991) describes gradual changes in cognitions in the group where they begin to perceive the victim as worthless and deserving of being bullied, resulting in the victim being even more rejected. It becomes the accepted social norm of the group to dislike the victim. As participant role theory views the peer group with a key role in bullying, a whole-school programme to address bullying needs to tackle not only the behaviour of the bullies, but also peer support for bullying by influencing the peer group to express disapproval of bullying and stand up for victims (Saarento et al., 2015).

Critical thinking task 5.1

Think back to your own experience at school and recall any examples of bullying you experienced or observed.
Try applying Salmivalli et al.'s six participant roles to your recollections.
Or apply Salmivalli et al.'s six participant roles to bullying in 'Mean Girls'.

Social information processing

The six-step **social information processing** model (Crick & Dodge, 1994) views aggressive bullying behaviour as resulting from a deficit in processing social information:

Social information processing Aggressive bullying behaviour is viewed as resulting from a deficit in perceiving, interpreting, retrieving, and processing social information.

Step 1 Perception and encoding of particular cues in a social situation. For example, another child passes in corridor, looking ahead of him, happily, and the bully perceives this as 'that kid is looking at me'. The bully is incorrectly perceiving the other's behaviour when they are just passing by.
Step 2 Biased interpretation of cues according to biased attribution. The bully tends to interpret others behaviour as hostile where there is ambiguity, 'he's laughing at me, he's disrespecting me'.
Step 3 Selection of antisocial behaviour, e.g. get even.
Step 4 Access behaviour from memory previous bullying responses to this or construct new ones.
Step 5 Evaluate possible responses from Step 4 and decide which to do.
Step 6 Enact chosen bullying behaviour.

Crick and Dodge's model has been highly influential in stimulating research but with some degree of controversy. Although aggressive behaviour is associated with deficits in social information processing, this may not necessarily apply to those who bully. Some studies have shown that it is victims of bullying who have a social information processing deficit and that bullies either have no deficit or superior social information processing (Guy et al., 2017; Sutton et al., 1999; Ziv et al., 2013).

Theory of mind

Picking up on the theme of bullies possessing superior social cognitive skills, one explanation is that bullies have a sophisticated **theory of mind**. Theory of mind is where you recognise that another person has a mental state, beliefs, emotions, and intentions that might not be the same as yours. You can use it to understand and predict another's behaviour. Good understanding of another is usually associated with

Theory of mind Recognising that another person has a mental state, beliefs, emotions, and intentions that might not be the same as yours.

prosocial behaviour, but, on the contrary, when applied to the study of bullying, is antisocial. Here, the bully is highly socially competent and understands very well how to interpret emotional cues from the victim about their feelings. The bully though puts these advanced social skills to use in antisocial ways to manipulate not only the victim but also to manipulate peers to participate in the bullying (Smith, 2016b, 2017; Sutton et al., 1999).

Critical thinking task 5.2

Repeat Critical thinking task 5.1 but this time applying theory of mind to your analysis of bullying observed or experienced.

Social identity theory

Social identity theory is the application of the work of Henri Tajfel (Tajfel et al., 1971; Tajfel & Turner, 1979) to the study of bullying in schools. Tajfel and colleagues recognised the importance to people of belonging to a group and that a group can give its members a positive social identity. This could be, for example, as supporters of a particular football team or members of a religious group, a family, or a school class. There are three key cognitive elements to a social identity evolving. People first *categorise* themselves as a member of the group and then *identify* with the group's values and goals, which can give them a sense of purpose and a sense of shared achievement. Norms for attitudes and behaviour are established within the group, and the expectation is that group members will conform to these. Finally, they *compare* their group with other groups, usually viewing members of their group more positively than members of another group. The group they belong to is the 'in-group'; others are in the

> **Social identity theory** Categorising yourself as a member of a group and identifying with that group are viewed as giving you a positive identity, influencing your self-esteem and self-concept. It also involves favourable comparisons of your group (in-group) with others (out-group).

'out-group'. Social identity theory has provided a useful model for subsequent research studies aimed at understanding the influence of groups and social processes on bullying in schools (e.g. Gini, 2007; Jones et al., 2012; Jones et al., 2008; Nesdale & Dalton, 2011; Nesdale & Lawson, 2011; Ojala & Nesdale, 2004)

Box 5.2 Case study: social identity theory research on bullying

Nesdale and Dalton's (2011) study explored whether the impact of the norms of a child's social groups might be moderated to improve the social environment of the class. 128 Australian children, 7-year-olds and 9-year-olds, from two schools, took part in this simulation study where children were allocated membership of a team based on drawings that they did. The in-group norm was manipulated according to how much the children were told to like or include children from outside their group. Alongside the group norm was a school norm that encouraged inclusiveness. The older group's attitudes on exclusion of the out-group were significantly moderated by the school norm, suggesting that the older children were more aware of the importance of listening to advice from adults about unacceptable behaviours. This simulation study was consistent with previous studies that found social group norms were strongly influential on the attitudes of young children towards other groups, but that this could be moderated by contrary school norms. This suggests a way forward for anti-bullying intervention strategies in schools.

Nesdale, D., & Dalton, D. (2011). Children's social groups and intergroup prejudice: assessing the influence and inhibition of social group norms. *British Journal of Developmental Psychology, 29*, 895–909.

Social dominance theory

Social dominance theory comes from animal behaviourist research, where there is typically a hierarchical pecking order in animals who live in packs. The strong oppress and dominate the weak. Unlike animals, school bullies are not competing for food or water but for dominance in the group, social approval, attention, or popularity (Hawley, 2014). By bullying a more vulnerable, less aggressive peer, they achieve dominance in the class hierarchy. They can also achieve popularity from the bystanders, reinforcers, and assistants who witness and facilitate the act of bullying (Pan et al., 2020). Criticisms of this theory view it as rather a bleak view of human nature, arguing that establishing a hierarchical structure which may be of practical use for a group is not the same as establishing social dominance with the purpose of oppressing those weaker (Turner & Reynolds, 2003).

Social dominance theory This theory proposes that societies maintain cohesion by creating a hierarchy where one social group is superior to, and dominates, others.

Theory of planned behaviour

The **theory of planned behaviour (TPB)** (Ajzen, 1991) has been applied extensively to study health behaviours such smoking, exercise, and dieting. It has been utilised to a lesser extent to study behaviour in a school setting, but has, for example, been found valuable for investigating teacher intentions and behaviour with respect to including children with special educational needs in mainstream classes (MacFarlane & Marks Woolfson, 2013; Urton et al., 2023; Wilson et al., 2016; Yan & Sin, 2015). The

Theory of planned behaviour To predict whether a particular behaviour will occur, factors to be considered are attitudes to that behaviour, subjective norm (others' attitudes to that behaviour), perceived behavioural control (how easy or difficult the behaviour is to perform), and behavioural intention (how strong is the intention to perform the behaviour).

theory examines the relationship between attitudes, intentions, and behaviours. Specifically, the TPB proposes that to predict whether a particular behaviour will occur, several factors need to be considered. What are the individual's *attitudes* towards that behaviour? What is the individual's perception of whether significant others will approve of that behaviour, *subjective norm*? How easy/difficult does the individual think it will be to perform the behaviour, *perceived behavioural control*? How willing is the individual to carry out the behaviour, *behavioural intention*? Behaviour is best predicted by behavioural intention which is itself predicted by attitudes, subjective norm, and perceived behavioural control. This theory aligns well with the multifactorial model for understanding violence proposed by World Health Organisation in 2020. Using an expanded version of the TPB, Jaber et al. (2023) found in their sample of 342 Canadian high school students that attitudes and beliefs about aggression predicted bullying behaviour. A positive practical implication of this finding for schools is that attitudes and beliefs can be changed through anti-bullying intervention. Pabian and Vandebosch (2014) applied the theory to cyberbullying, with 1606 Belgian high school students. Their findings showed that intention to engage in cyberbullying was a predictor of cyberbullying behaviour.

Summary

This chapter is a companion to Chapter 4 in its coverage of social psychological theories that have been applied in educational psychology. Here though, we examined social theories that educational psychology practitioners and researchers use to understand the specific phenomenon of bullying in schools. This is recognised internationally as a serious social problem with long-term effects on victims. Educational psychologists use these theoretical insights to develop anti-bullying intervention programmes. These will be addressed in Chapter 10.

References/Further reading

Ajzen, I. (1991). The theory of planned behavior. *Organizational Behavior and Human Decision Processes*, *50*(2), 179–211.

Bandura, A. (1973). *Aggression: A social learning analysis*. Prentice-Hall.

Bussey, K. (2023). The contribution of social cognitive theory to school bullying research and practice. *Theory into Practice*, *62*(3), 293–305. https://doi.org/10.1080/00405841.2023.2226549

Crick, N. R., & Dodge, K. A. (1994). A review and reformulation of social information-processing mechanisms in children's social adjustment. *Psychological Bulletin*, *115*(1), 74.

Del Rey, R., Espino, E., Ojeda, M., & Mora-Merchán, J. A. (2022). Bullying. In P. Smith & C. Hart (Eds.), *The Wiley-Blackwell handbook of childhood social development* (pp. 591–608). Wiley-Blackwell.

Earnshaw, V. A., Reisner, S. L., Menino, D. D., Poteat, V. P., Bogart, L. M., Barnes, T. N., & Schuster, M. A. (2018). Stigma-based bullying interventions: A systematic review. *Developmental Review*, *48*, 178–200 (Developmental Review).

Gini, G. (2007). Who is blameworthy?: Social identity and inter-group bullying. *School Psychology International*, *28*(1), 77–89.

Gönültaş, S., & Mulvey, K. L. (2021). The role of immigration background, intergroup processes, and social-cognitive skills in bystanders' responses to bias-based bullying toward immigrants during adolescence. *Child Development*, *92*(3), e296–e316 (Child Development).

Guy, A., Lee, K., & Wolke, D. (2017). Differences in the early stages of social information processing for adolescents involved in bullying. *Aggressive Behavior*, *43*(6), 578–587. https://doi.org/https://doi.org/10.1002/ab.21716

Hawley, P. H. (2014). Ontogeny and social dominance: A developmental view of human power patterns. *Evolutionary Psychology*, *12*(2), 318–342.

Jaber, L. S., Rinaldi, C. M., Saunders, C. D., & Scott, J. (2023). The intent behind bullying: An application and expansion of the theory of planned behaviour. *Contemporary School Psychology*, *27*(3), 411–425. https://doi.org/10.1007/s40688-021-00403-3

Jetelina, K. K., Reingle Gonzalez, J. M., Cuccaro, P. M., Peskin, M. F., Pompeii, L., Atem, F. ... Schuster, M. A. (2019). Self-reporting discrepancies of bullying victimization and perpetration measures. *Annals of Epidemiology*, *32*, 58–63. https://doi.org/https://doi.org/10.1016/j.annepidem.2019.01.008

Jones, S. E., Bombieri, L., Livingstone, A. G., & Manstead, A. S. R. (2012). The influence of norms and social identities on children's responses to bullying. *British Journal of Educational Psychology*, *82*(2), 241–256.

Jones, S. E., Haslam, S. A., York, L., & Ryan, M. K. (2008). Rotten apple or rotten barrel? Social identity and children's responses to bullying. *British Journal of Developmental Psychology*, *26*(1), 117–132. https://doi.org/https://doi.org/10.1348/026151007X200385

MacFarlane, K., & Marks Woolfson, L. (2013). Teacher attitudes and behavior toward the inclusion of children with social, emotional and behavioral difficulties in mainstream schools: An application of the theory of planned behavior. *Teaching and Teacher Education*, *29*, 46–52. https://doi.org/https://doi.org/10.1016/j.tate.2012.08.006 (Teaching and Teacher Education).

Nesdale, D., & Dalton, D. (2011). Children's social groups and intergroup prejudice: Assessing the influence and inhibition of social group norms. *British Journal of Developmental Psychology*, *29*(4), 895–909. https://doi.org/https://doi.org/10.1111/j.2044-835X.2010.02017.x

Nesdale, D., & Lawson, M. J. (2011). Social groups and children's intergroup attitudes: Can school norms moderate the effects of social group norms? *Child Development*, *82*(5), 1594–1606. https://doi.org/https://doi.org/10.1111/j.1467-8624.2011.01637.x

Ojala, K., & Nesdale, D. (2004). Bullying and social identity: The effects of group norms and distinctiveness threat on attitudes towards bullying. *British Journal of Developmental Psychology*, *22*(1), 19–35. https://doi.org/https://doi.org/10.1348/026151004772901096

Olweus, D. (1991). Victimization among school children. *Advances in Psychology*, *76*, 45–102.

Pabian, S., & Vandebosch, H. (2014). Using the theory of planned behaviour to understand cyberbullying: The importance of beliefs for developing interventions. *European Journal of Developmental Psychology*, *11*(4), 463–477.

Pan, B., Zhang, L., Ji, L., Garandeau, C. F., Salmivalli, C., & Zhang, W. (2020). Classroom status hierarchy moderates the association between social dominance goals and bullying behavior in middle childhood and early adolescence. *Journal of Youth and Adolescence*, *49*(11), 2285–2297. https://doi.org/10.1007/s10964-020-01285-z (Journal of Youth and Adolescence).

Pepler, D., Craig, W., & O'Connell, P. (2009). Peer processes in bullying: Informing prevention and intervention strategies. In *Handbook of bullying in schools* (pp. 469–478). Routledge.

Rivers, I., & Smith, P. K. (1994). Types of bullying behaviour and their correlates. *Aggressive Behavior*, *20*(5), 359–368.

Saarento, S., Boulton, A. J., & Salmivalli, C. (2015). Reducing bullying and victimization: Student- and classroom-level mechanisms of change. *Journal of Abnormal Child Psychology*, *43*, 61–76.

Salmivalli, C., Lagerspetz, K., Björkqvist, K., Österman, K., & Kaukiainen, A. (1996). Bullying as a group process: Participant roles and their relations to social status within the group. *Aggressive*

Behavior: Official Journal of the International Society for Research on Aggression, *22*(1), 1–15.

Smith, P. K. (2016a). Bullying: Definition, types, causes, consequences and intervention. *Social and Personality Psychology Compass*, *10*(9), 519–532.

Smith, P. K. (2016b). Research and practice in the study of school bullying. In K. Durkin & H. Schaffer (Eds.), *The Wiley handbook of developmental psychology in practice: Implementation and impact* (pp. 290–310). John Wiley & Sons.

Smith, P. K. (2017). Bullying and theory of mind: A review. *Current Psychiatry Reviews*, *13*(2), 90–95.

Smith, P. K. (2023). The research program on school bullying: How and why it has developed over the last 50 years. *Vernon Wall Lectures* (41).

Smith, P. K., & Sharp, S. (Eds.). (2002). *School bullying: Insights and perspectives.* Routledge.

Sutton, J., Smith, P. K., & Swettenham, J. (1999). Bullying and 'theory of mind': A critique of the 'social skills deficit' view of anti-social behaviour. *Social Development*, *8*(1), 117–127. https://doi.org/https://doi.org/10.1111/1467-9507.00083

Swearer, S. M., Wang, C., Berry, B., & Myers, Z. R. (2014). Reducing bullying: Application of social cognitive theory. *Theory into Practice*, *53*(4), 271–277. https://doi.org/10.1080/00405841.2014.947221

Tajfel, H., Billig, M. G., Bundy, R. P., & Flament, C. (1971). Social categorization and intergroup behaviour. *European Journal of Social Psychology*, *1*(2), 149–178.

Tajfel, H., & Turner, J. (1979). An integrative theory of intergroup conflict. In W. Austin & S. Worchel (Eds.), *The social psychology of intergroup relations* (pp. 56–65). Brooks/Cole.

Turner, J. C., & Reynolds, K. J. (2003). Why social dominance theory has been falsified. *British Journal of Social Psychology*, *42*(2), 199–206. https://doi.org/https://doi.org/10.1348/014466603322127184 (British Journal of Social Psychology).

Urton, K., Wilbert, J., Krull, J., & Hennemann, T. (2023). Factors explaining teachers' intention to implement inclusive practices in the classroom: Indications based on the theory of planned behaviour. *Teaching and Teacher Education*, *132*, 104225.

Wilson, C., Marks Woolfson, L., Durkin, K., & Elliott, M. A. (2016). The impact of social cognitive and personality factors on teachers' reported inclusive behaviour. *British Journal of Educational Psychology*, *86*(3), 461–480.

Yan, Z., & Sin, K.-f. (2015). Exploring the intentions and practices of principals regarding inclusive education: An application of the Theory of Planned Behaviour. *Cambridge Journal of Education*, *45*(2), 205–221.

Ziv, Y., Leibovich, I., & Shechtman, Z. (2013). Bullying and victimization in early adolescence: Relations to social information processing patterns. *Aggressive Behavior*, *39*(6), 482–492.

Chapter 6

Mental health and wellbeing in school

In the previous chapter, we discussed whole-school approaches to bullying with the aim of schools creating a positive school environment that will allow all children to feel safe and to thrive. In this chapter, we will examine theories that educational psychology uses that contribute to building such an environment. In particular, we look at theories that have a positive view of the human capacity to strive to achieve potential and solve their own problems. The chapter will explore how these theories help teachers create classrooms that promote child mental health and wellbeing by being a safe and emotionally warm environment that supports children to explore ideas, make mistakes, and achieve their potential.

Humanistic psychology

You may see **humanistic psychology** referred to as the 'Third Force in Psychology', behaviourism and psychoanalytic psychology being the first two 'forces' in psychology. Some felt that these first two psychologies had led to the loss of an essential human element. There began to be an interest in understanding

> **Humanistic psychology** This views people as having free will, capable of change, and having the potential to strive towards personal fulfilment and meaningful lives.

DOI: 10.4324/9781032691541-8

the human condition in a more **holistic** way and particularly how to develop its potential. Humanistic psychologists have an optimistic view of people that they have free will, are capable of change, and strive towards personal fulfilment and meaningful lives. Humanistic psychology principles and values have not only influenced approaches to psychotherapy and counselling, but also education and parenting practices.

Holistic This perspective considers that psychological study of specific variables does not sufficiently lead to understanding the human experience. To do this, psychology needs to study the person as a whole.

Maslow's self-actualisation Abraham Maslow's theory has been, and still is, highly influential. He proposed that all humans are motivated to strive for **self-actualisation**, reaching their potential at the highest possible level. He viewed self-actualisation as at the apex of a pyramid hierarchy of human motivational needs, with basic physiological needs of shelter, food, and sleep at the bottom, with safety and security needs next. Next comes psychological needs such as love and belongingness, family, and friendship; and esteem needs such as recognition, appreciation, achievement, and respect. Finally self-actualisation needs are at the top of the hierarchy pyramid. They are experienced as finding meaning and personal fulfilment in life, perhaps through your work, creativity, sport, volunteering, interests, and being the person you can be in whatever way is important to you.

Self-actualisation Finding meaning and personal fulfilment in life, being the person you are capable of being in whatever way is important to you.

Maslow's original conceptualisation was that needs higher up the hierarchy can only be met once lower down needs are met (Maslow, 1954). You aren't in a position to strive towards personal achievements when you are lacking food and water. Your motivational goals would be directed towards getting these basic needs met. In the third edition of his book in 1987, Maslow clarified that these levels are not in a rigid sequence and that a lower-level need would not have to be fully satisfied before a person could be motivated towards the next-level motivational goals. Most people are likely to be partly satisfied in all levels and partly dissatisfied at all levels of the hierarchy, but perhaps almost fully satisfied at the level of basic physiological needs and safety needs, less satisfied in belongingness, and even less in esteem, and least of all in self-fulfilment needs.

Another way of viewing this hierarchy is through the lens of intrinsic and extrinsic motivation. The lower section of the hierarchy comprises extrinsic motivation where goals such as food and recognition are external to us. The top section motivational goals of fulfilment are internal. Intrinsic goals are those that we strive towards because we enjoy and value them. They do not bring extrinsic rewards such as recognition of achievement, or high grades, but instead we find them absorbing and engaging in themselves.

Humanistic educators aim for student-centred, self-directed classroom activities in which students can find personal meaning and engage in with real interest and enthusiasm for learning. They take a holistic approach to the purpose of education so are concerned not only with the academic aspect of students' school experience but also their emotional wellbeing and mental health, to help learners strive towards self-actualisation (DeRobertis, 2013). They recognise a relationship between deficiency needs where children lack food or security and higher-level growth needs of academic achievement (Noltemeyer et al., 2012).

Maslow's hierarchy has influenced policies internationally with governments acknowledging that children are not ready to learn if they come to school hungry, so schools in areas of poverty and deprivation often provide breakfast clubs to address this basic physiological need. While there is some evidence that supports the sequential order of the hierarchy (Compton, 2024), there is also research evidence that doesn't and that suggests that policies should not therefore prioritise one need level before others (Rojas et al., 2023). It has also been proposed that perhaps Maslow's hierarchical sequence explains needs more effectively at the level of culture and society, with daily food intake, safety from war, low divorce rates, women in workforce, and enrolment in university education as societal quality of life markers of the pyramid levels (Hagerty, 1999).

Critical thinking task 6.1

How can understanding Maslow's hierarchy of needs help schools improve children's mental health?

Rogers core conditions Carl Rogers was a psychotherapist who developed a **non-directive**, person-centred approach to working with his clients. Unlike Maslow who viewed self-actualisation as only achievable by the few when other lower-level needs were in the main satisfied, Rogers saw self-actualisation as innate and as the motivational driver for everyone's behaviour. Rogers (1957) proposed that for a person to be fully functioning, to achieve self-actualisation through psychotherapy, six conditions were both necessary and sufficient. These were later distilled to three core conditions that need to be provided by the therapist to ensure a quality relationship with the client.

> **Non-directive approach** The counsellor doesn't direct the sessions by having a therapeutic agenda or particular goals. Instead, the counsellor establishes a supportive relationship to help the client to clarify their ideas, feelings, and goals.

Congruence Effective therapists demonstrate **congruence** by being genuine, authentic and open in the therapist role. They are their real selves in the therapeutic relationship. They do not adopt a guarded, professional, powerful, knowing, mysterious persona, but instead are able to share relevant feelings and reactions (Mearns et al., 2013; Rogers, 2012; Rogers, 1995)

> **Congruence** Therapists are their real selves in the therapeutic relationship and can express feelings that are relevant to the situation.

Empathy This is not the same as sympathy.

> **Empathy** This involves understanding the client's world as they perceive it.

Empathy involves understanding the client's world as they perceive it. Empathy requires listening very carefully not only to what the client is saying verbally but also what they are communicating through their body language. It involves recognising the deep meaning in what is said, in particular picking up on emotion and not just the surface meaning of the words spoken. Accurate empathy can be demonstrated by reflecting back to the client the thoughts and feelings they have expressed, showing the client that they are understood (Gillon, 2007; Rogers, 2012; Rogers, 1995).

Unconditional positive regard The therapist views the client positively, accepts them with warmth and without judgement, and demonstrates an attitude of caring. Furthermore, this is **unconditional positive regard** because it is not dependent on liking either the client or the client's opinions (Mearns et al., 2013; Rogers, 2012; Rogers, 1995).

Unconditional positive regard Viewing the client positively, accepting them with warmth and without judgement, and demonstrating an attitude of caring, regardless of the client's behaviour or opinions.

What then is the link between person-centred psychology and education? Not only did Rogers view these core conditions as necessary for psychotherapeutic relationships but also as necessary conditions for other relationships that aim to facilitate individuals to achieve their potential. Applying these ideas to teaching and learning, he viewed effective relationships at the heart of successful classrooms, where teachers create a warm, non-judgemental classroom atmosphere, in which they collaborate with learners through experiential learning, to help them reach their own learning goals. Teachers in such a classroom are their authentic selves and show empathy towards their students who feel acknowledged and understood by their teacher. In order to achieve feelings of self-worth, children need to experience unconditional positive regard from their teachers, as well as from parents and other significant adults in their lives (Rogers et al., 2013; Rogers & Freiberg, 1994). In addition, person-centred counselling is a frequently used intervention to provide psychological support in school to young people who are experiencing mental health difficulties, especially in the UK (Cooper et al., 2014).

Critical thinking task 6.2

Think about your own experiences in school.
In which teachers' classes did you experience Rogers' core conditions?

Although Carl Rogers died in 1987, the legacy of his work continues with a high volume of published books and papers on the topic and a multiplicity of person-centred training courses. Furthermore, there is now a considerable body of supporting research evidence (Elliott, 2002; Kirschenbaum & Jourdan, 2005; Murphy & Joseph, 2016).

Online resource 6.1 The humanist teacher
Helpful professor explains (2023). Humanism in education. Are you a humanist teacher? 16 October. Available at: www.youtube.com/watch?v=0_aOCgJaZPA (Accessed: 28 February 2025).

Positive psychology

The term **positive psychology** was first coined by Maslow (1954) as the title of a chapter in his seminal book *Motivation and Personality*. Indeed, even earlier than this, William James, whose contribution to educational psychology we discussed in Chapter 1, questioned why there were individuals who were able to attain optimal functioning and others not. But it is Martin Seligman who is usually considered as the 'father' of positive psychology. Like humanistic psychology, positive psychology is focused not on addressing psychological weakness or deficiency, mental illness, or psychopathology, but rather on how healthy individuals achieve personal growth and self-actualisation. Although both approaches share the goal of promoting human wellbeing, the two differ significantly in philosophical underpinnings, research methodologies, and counselling interventions (Waterman, 2013).

Positive psychology This is about enhancing subjective experiences such as wellbeing and happiness, optimism for the future, and personal traits like perseverance.

Seligman (2002) describes positive psychology as being about subjective experiences such as wellbeing and happiness, optimism for the future, and personal traits like perseverance and forgiveness. At group level it is about institutions that promote civic values such as responsibility, tolerance, altruism, and work ethic. Seligman (2011) proposed five permanent building blocks for a fulfilling life, using the acronym PERMA:

Positive emotion Examples of this are gratitude, love, joy, happiness, and hope. These relate to emotions about the past, the here and now, and emotions regarding the future

Engagement This is where you are fully absorbed in an activity that provides just the right amount of challenge for your strengths and abilities. It results in 'flow' which is an optimally satisfying experience resulting in deep concentration and enjoyment (Csikszentmihalyi & Csikzentmihaly, 1990; Csikszentmihalyi & LeFevre, 1989).

Relationships This building block is seen as crucial for wellbeing. It includes all the relationships in your life, with family, friends, and colleagues. They give our lives meaning and provide a pathway through which we can feel loved and valued, through which we can share laughter and joy and be supported when times are difficult.

Meaning The task of finding meaning in life can be through family, career, volunteering, religion, creativity, and hobbies. It gives your life purpose and gives you a sense of being part of something more important than yourself.

Accomplishment This is a sense of achievement or mastery, of being motivated and persevering towards reaching a goal. This can, for example, be through work, or hobbies, or sports, but also through many other spheres of activity.

Online resource 6.2 PERMA explained

Be Well Co (2015). Prof Seligman on PERMA. 7 April. Available at: www.youtube.com/watch?v=jqqHUxzpfBI (Accessed: 28 February 2025).

Online resource 6.3 Link to Prof Seligman's Authentic Happiness website at University of Pennsylvania with multiple resources
www.authentichappiness.sas.upenn.edu/ (Accessed: 28 February 2025).

Seligman proposed that wellbeing comprised high levels of each of the PERMA building blocks. Thus to improve wellbeing, interventions should target the building block elements (Seligman, 2018). The PERMA model has been applied to wellbeing in a range of areas that include wellbeing at work (Yang et al., 2022) and in university students (Kovich et al., 2023), mental illness in war veterans (Umucu, 2021), and resilience and mental health in children (Turner et al., 2023). The model has been applied internationally in research studies on wellbeing beyond the United States, including Brazil (de Carvalho et al., 2023), Germany (Wammerl et al., 2019), Turkey (Ayse, 2018), (Ryan et al., 2019), and United Arab Emirates (Lambert D'raven & Pasha-Zaidi, 2016). PERMA changed from being a definition of wellbeing to being antecedents of wellbeing and not an exhaustive list of antecedents (Cabrera & Donaldson, 2024). This led to other building blocks being added to the model. In 2020, four new building blocks were added: physical health, economic security, mindset, and environment, with the researchers Donaldson and Donaldson (2020) recommending this PERMA+4 as a more holistic framework, especially for the world of work and reporting it to be useful predictor of wellbeing.

Positive psychology in the classroom

Educational psychologists, both practitioners and researchers, began to be interested in applying **positive psychology** to school children. In 2004, a special edition of the journal Psychology in the Schools was devoted to positive psychology; Chafouleas and Bray (2004) argued here that rather than school psychologists focusing on trying to improve deficits in children's behaviour and learning, positive psychology should be applied to schools too. Over the following 20 years, there has been a great increase in research papers examining relationships between PERMA and PERMA+4 elements and wellbeing, positive functioning, mental health, and resilience (Cabrera & Donaldson, 2024; Turner et al., 2023).

Online resource 6.4 Positive psychology in the classroom
The Brainwaves video anthology (2017). Martin Seligman – positive education. Are you a humanist teacher? 11 May. Available at: www.youtube.com/watch?v=igpqyuw6GLw (Accessed: 28 February 2025).

Box 6.1 Applying theory to practice for educators: Geelong Grammar School's whole-school approach to positive education

Research studies outside the school context have shown that wellbeing influences life satisfaction, physical health, depression, and learning. This led to the idea that wellbeing could and should be taught in school. Two positive education programmes that Seligman and his team tested out (2009) are the Penn Resiliency Programme (PRP) and the Positive Psychology Programme.

The PRP comprises 18 lessons of 90 minutes scheduled in the school day delivered to children aged 10–14 years old. It aims to teach children the skills of how to cope with everyday stressors and build resilience and optimistic thinking. It does this by role play, quizzes, group activities, and discussion of scenarios. It is usually delivered by teachers, but can also be delivered by teaching assistants, school counsellors, educational psychologists, or social workers. It works best though if the group leader has undertaken PRP training. Research findings show that PRP reduces and prevents symptoms of depression and anxiety, reduces hopelessness, and works equally well across different ethnic backgrounds.

The Positive Psychology Programme aims to build resilience and develop the PERMA elements, positive emotion, and sense of purpose. Examples of activities used in the sessions are writing down three good things that have happened each day for a week and reflecting as to why they happened, why they felt good, and how can you have them happening more often. Another activity involves asking students to identify their character strengths, for example, kindness, perseverance, and then working out how to increase their use of these in school and with friends and family. Seligman et al. reported students on the programme increased their enjoyment and engagement in learning.

Only class groups took part in the above programmes. The Geelong Grammar School project was the first whole-school positive education project for Seligman et al. (2009). This is a four-campus school near Melbourne. Its holistic approach promotes positive education values throughout the school with courses for Years 9 and 10 that explicitly teach PERMA elements. Elements of positive education are further embedded within classes, for example, in English when discussing novels and in geography examining the happiness of a nation. All teaching and support staff take part in a three-day training programme. Outcomes recently published by Rickard et al. (2024) reported higher levels of life satisfaction and social relatedness compared to the comparison group from other schools. It was noted though that the effect size was small. The authors suggest this may partly have been due to the high quality of the comparison social–emotional programme and that it may also have partly evolved into a positive education programme as they were not 'blinded' to the purpose of the study.

Solution-focused psychology

Solution-focused psychology An that focuses on setting goals for the future and building solutions on past successes.

Solution-focused psychology has been a popular approach with practitioner educational psychologists for the last 30 years (Stobie et al., 2005). It belongs here because it aligns well with this chapter's focus on the human capacity for dealing positively with problems and solving their own difficulties.

Indeed, it has been suggested that solution-focused psychology could even provide a practical coaching base for implementing positive psychology theory (Terni, 2015)

Solution-focused therapy was developed by Steve de Shazer at the Milwaukee Brief Family Therapy Centre in the early 1980s (de Shazer, 1985). Rather than concentrating therapeutic intervention on the past and on understanding the problem, solution-focused psychology focuses on setting goals for the future and building solutions on past successes. The miracle question is one of the key components of this approach where the client is asked if a miracle happened and the problem was solved, how would you know, and what would be different? (de Shazer, 1988).

Online resource 6.5 The miracle question in counselling
Therapy solutions (2022). The miracle question. 4 April. Available at: www.youtube.com/watch?v=oG5AVk-5SH0 (Accessed: 28 February 2025).

This approach originally used by psychotherapists and counsellors was adopted by education professionals and adapted to the school context. Practitioner educational psychologists found that it could be applied to individual children, families, and class groups and was sufficiently flexible to be useful in assessment, prevention, intervention, key areas of their work (Ajmal, 1995). It has been applied to different areas, including organisational change (Morgan, 2016), bullying (Kvarme et al., 2013; Young & Holdorf, 2003), behaviour (James, 2016), and classroom relationships (Fernie & Cubeddu, 2016). Bond et al. (2013) reviewed 38 studies, mostly of solution-focused practice applied to child behaviour problems and reported tentative support for its effectiveness, particularly in the early stages of a developing problem. Solution-focused work is now an established part of the practice of professional educational psychologists (Harker et al., 2017).

Summary

The three theories covered in this chapter have particularly influenced professional educational psychologists in their work with children and young people, their families, and the education staff working with them. At the level of individual mental health difficulties, these theories show respect for problem owners by recognising their capacity for solving their own difficulties and achieving their potential. Each theory here provided a different way of facilitating that process. At the class or school level, they aim to provide warm, supportive learning environments in which children can thrive.

References/Further reading

Ajmal, Y. R. J. (1995). Solution-focused brief therapy, EPs and schools. *Educational and Child Psychology*, *12*(12), 16–21. https://doi.org/10.53841/bpsecp.1995.12.4.16

Ayse, E. B. (2018). Adaptation of the PERMA well-being scale into Turkish: Validity and reliability studies. *Educational Research and Reviews*, *13*(4), 129–135.

Bond, C., Woods, K., Humphrey, N., Symes, W., & Green, L. (2013). Practitioner Review: The effectiveness of solution focused brief therapy with children and families: A systematic and critical evaluation of the literature from 1990–2010. *Journal of Child Psychology and Psychiatry*, *54*(7), 707–723. https://doi.org/https://doi.org/10.1111/jcpp.12058

Cabrera, V., & Donaldson, S. I. (2024). PERMA to PERMA+ 4 building blocks of well-being: A systematic review of the empirical literature. *The Journal of Positive Psychology*, *19*(3), 510–529.

Chafouleas, S. M., & Bray, M. A. (2004). Introducing positive psychology: Finding a place within school psychology. *Psychology in the Schools*, *41*(1), 1–5.

Compton, W. C. (2024). Self-actualization myths: What did Maslow really say? *Journal of Humanistic Psychology*, *64*(5), 743–760.

Cooper, M., McGinnis, S., & Carrick, L. (2014). School-based humanistic counselling for psychological distress in young people: A practice research network to address the attrition problem. *Counselling & Psychotherapy Research*, *14*(3), 201–211. https://doi.org/10.1080/14733145.2014.929415

Csikszentmihalyi, M., & Csikzentmihaly, M. (1990). *Flow: The psychology of optimal experience* (Vol. 1990). Harper & Row New York.

Csikszentmihalyi, M., & LeFevre, J. (1989). Optimal experience in work and leisure. *Journal of Personality and Social Psychology*, *56*(5), 815.

de Carvalho, T. F., de Aquino, S. D., & Natividade, J. C. (2023). Flourishing in the Brazilian context: Evidence of the validity of the

PERMA-profiler scale. *Current Psychology*, *42*(3), 1828–1840. https://doi.org/10.1007/s12144-021-01587-w
de Shazer, S. (1985). *Keys to solution in brief therapy*. Norton.
de Shazer, S. (1988). *Clues: Investigating solutions in brief therapy*. Norton.
DeRobertis, E. M. (2013). Humanistic psychology: Alive in the 21st century? *Journal of Humanistic Psychology*, *53*(4), 419–437.
Donaldson, S. I., & Donaldson, S. I. (2020). The positive functioning at work scale: Psychometric assessment, validation, and measurement invariance. *Journal of Well-Being Assessment*, *4*(2), 181–215.
Elliott, R. (2002). The effectiveness of humanistic therapies: A meta-analysis. In *Humanistic psychotherapies: Handbook of research and practice* (pp. 57–81). American Psychological Association. https://doi.org/10.1037/10439-002
Fernie, L., & Cubeddu, D. (2016). WOWW: A solution orientated approach to enhance classroom relationships and behaviour within a primary three class. *Educational Psychology in Practice*, *32*(2), 197–208.
Gillon, E. (2007). *Person-centred counselling psychology: An introduction*. Sage.
Hagerty, M. R. (1999). Testing Maslow's hierarchy of needs: National quality-of-life across time. *Social Indicators Research*, *46*(3), 249–271. https://doi.org/10.1023/A:1006921107298
Harker, M. E., Dean, S., & Monsen, J. J. (2017). Solution-oriented educational psychology practice. In *Frameworks for practice in educational psychology: A textbook for trainees and practitioners. Second edition* (pp. 167–193). Jessica Kingsley.
James, G. (2016). *Transforming behaviour in the classroom: A solution-focused guide for new teachers*. Sage.
Kirschenbaum, H., & Jourdan, A. (2005). The current status of Carl Rogers and the person-centered approach. *Psychotherapy: Theory, Research, Practice, Training*, *42*(1), 37–51. https://doi.org/10.1037/0033-3204.42.1.37
Kovich, M. K., Simpson, V. L., Foli, K. J., Hass, Z., & Phillips, R. G. (2023). Application of the PERMA model of well-being in undergraduate students. *International Journal of Community Well-Being*, *6*(1), 1–20.
Kvarme, L. G., Aabø, L. S., & Sæteren, B. (2013). "I feel I mean something to someone": Solution-focused brief therapy support groups for bullied schoolchildren. *Educational Psychology in Practice*, *29*(4), 416–431.
Lambert D'raven, L., & Pasha-Zaidi, N. (2016). Using the PERMA model in the United Arab Emirates. *Social Indicators Research*, *125*, 905–933.

Maslow, A. (1954). *Motivation and personality*. Harpers.

Mearns, D., McLeod, J., & Thorne, B. (2013). *Person-centred counselling in action*. Sage.

Morgan, G. (2016). Organisational change: A solution-focused approach. *Educational Psychology in Practice*, *32*(2), 133–144.

Murphy, D., & Joseph, S. (2016). Person-centered therapy: Past, present, and future orientations. In *Humanistic psychotherapies: Handbook of research and practice, 2nd ed.* (pp. 185–218). American Psychological Association. https://doi.org/10.1037/14775-007

Noltemeyer, A., Bush, K., Patton, J., & Bergen, D. (2012). The relationship among deficiency needs and growth needs: An empirical investigation of Maslow's theory. *Children and Youth Services Review*, *34*(9), 1862–1867. https://doi.org/https://doi.org/10.1016/j.childyouth.2012.05.021

Rickard, N. S., Chin, T.-C., Cross, D., Hattie, J., & Vella-Brodrick, D. A. (2024). Effects of a positive education programme on secondary school students' mental health and wellbeing; challenges of the school context. *Oxford Review of Education*, *50*(3), 309–331.

Rogers, C. (2012). *Client centered therapy (new ed)*. Hachette UK.

Rogers, C., Lyon, H., & Tausch, R. (2013). *On becoming an effective teacher: Person-centered teaching, psychology, philosophy, and dialogues with Carl R. Rogers and Harold Lyon*. Routledge.

Rogers, C. R. (1957). The necessary and sufficient conditions of therapeutic personality change. *Journal of Consulting Psychology*, *21*(2), 95.

Rogers, C. R. (1995). *On becoming a person: A therapist's view of psychotherapy*. Houghton Mifflin Harcourt.

Rogers, C. R., & Freiberg, H. J. (1994). *Freedom to learn*. Merrill/Macmillan College Publishing Co.

Rojas, M., Méndez, A., & Watkins-Fassler, K. (2023). The hierarchy of needs empirical examination of Maslow's theory and lessons for development. *World Development*, *165*, 106185.

Ryan, J., Curtis, R., Olds, T., Edney, S., Vandelanotte, C., Plotnikoff, R., & Maher, C. (2019). Psychometric properties of the PERMA Profiler for measuring wellbeing in Australian adults. *PloS one*, *14*(12), e0225932.

Seligman, M. (2018). PERMA and the building blocks of well-being. *The Journal of Positive Psychology*, *13*(4), 333–335.

Seligman, M. E. (2002). Positive psychology, positive prevention, and positive therapy. In C. Snyder & S. Lopez (Eds.), *Handbook of positive psychology* (Vol. 2, pp. 3–12). Oxford University Press.

Seligman, M. E. (2011). *Flourish: A visionary new understanding of happiness and well-being*. Simon and Schuster.

Seligman, M. E., Ernst, R. M., Gillham, J., Reivich, K., & Linkins, M. (2009). Positive education: Positive psychology and classroom interventions. *Oxford Review of Education*, *35*(3), 293–311.

Stobie, I., Boyle, J., & Marks Woolfson, L. (2005). Solution-focused approaches in the practice of UK educational psychologists: A study of the nature of their application and evidence of their effectiveness. *School Psychology International*, *26*(1), 5–28.

Terni, P. (2015). Solution-focus: Bringing positive psychology into the conversation. *International Journal of Solution-Focused Practices*, *3*(1), 8–16.

Turner, J., Roberts, R., Proeve, M., & Chen, J. (2023). Relationship between PERMA and children's wellbeing, resilience and mental health: A scoping review. *International Journal of Wellbeing*, *13*(2).

Umucu, E. (2021). Examining the structure of the PERMA theory of well-being in veterans with mental illnesses. *Rehabilitation Counseling Bulletin*, *64*(4), 244–247.

Wammerl, M., Jaunig, J., Mairunteregger, T., & Streit, P. (2019). The German Version of the PERMA-Profiler: Evidence for construct and convergent validity of the PERMA theory of well-being in German speaking countries. *Journal of Well-Being Assessment*, *3*(2), 75–96. https://doi.org/10.1007/s41543-019-00021-0

Waterman, A. S. (2013). The humanistic psychology–positive psychology divide: Contrasts in philosophical foundations. *American Psychologist*, *68*(3), 124.

Yang, C.-C., Watanabe, K., & Kawakami, N. (2022). The associations between job strain, workplace PERMA profiler, and work engagement. *Journal of Occupational and Environmental Medicine*, *64*(5), 409–415.

Young, S., & Holdorf, G. (2003). Using solution focused brief therapy in individual referrals for bullying. *Educational Psychology in Practice*, *19*(4), 271–282.

[illegible] R. M. [illegible] Reivich, K. [illegible] psychology and [illegible] *[illegible] education*, [illegible] 293–311.

S[illegible] (2015). [illegible] practice: The [illegible] application and evidence of [illegible] *[illegible] Journal*, [illegible] 5–28.

[illegible]

[illegible] of [illegible] wellbeing [illegible]

[illegible] S. (201[illegible]). [illegible] positive psychology [illegible] *American [illegible]*

[illegible] N. (20[illegible]). [illegible]

[illegible]

Section 3

Key methodologies

This section in summary

Chapter 7

- Measuring quantifiable intervention outcomes
  - o What's an intervention?
  - o Standardised tests
  - o Surveys
  - o Sociometric analysis
- Commonly used research designs
  - o One-group pre-test post-test design
  - o Quasi-experimental design
  - o Single-case experimental design
- Did the intervention cause the outcome?
  - o Threats to internal validity

Chapter 8

- Qualitative methods
  - o Interviews
  - o Classroom observation
  - o Document analysis
  - o Criteria for evaluating qualitative research
- Mixed quantitative and qualitative methods research

DOI: 10.4324/9781032691541-9

Chapter 9

- Correlation is not causation
- Efficacy vs. effectiveness
- Statistical significance vs. clinical significance
- Implementation science
- Hierarchy of research designs

Chapter 7

Quantitative methods commonly used in real-world educational psychology research in schools

Medicine and other health professions, such as physiotherapy and occupational therapy, were leaders in recognising the importance of drawing up practice guidelines based on sound scientific research evidence, so that patients could receive treatment interventions that were known to work (Kratochwill, 2007). Over the last 25 years, professional educational psychologists have taken on board the importance of applying evidence-based practice in their work in schools (Frederickson, 2002). In common with the wider field of psychology, the discipline of educational psychology has been committed to scientific methods as optimal sources of evidence for application in the real world of the school, rather than relying solely on intuition, professional experience, or common sense (Lilienfeld et al., 2012). This chapter discusses the use of quantitative methodologies in educational psychology. It critically examines the extent to which some commonly used methods for classroom research can be considered to provide evidence of what works.

Measuring quantifiable intervention outcomes

What's an intervention?

The term **intervention** in educational psychology covers a wide range from therapeutic treatment with an individual, teacher classroom practices for managing behaviour,

Intervention Small- or large-scale action taken to improve a presenting problem in an individual or group.

DOI: 10.4324/9781032691541-10

a programme for improving literacy across a school, and a district's bullying policy. An intervention may be local and small-scale where an individual psychologist or educator acts systematically to improve a presenting problem with an individual, a class, and a school. Or it may be larger scale across a whole-school district or nationally or internationally, involving a team of researchers. It may make use of an established programme such as the widely used Incredible Years Parenting Programme (Webster-Stratton et al., 2011), or it may be more exploratory where one school tried out alternative sanctions to withdrawal of playtime (Clements & Harding, 2023). These are all interventions.

Both educational psychology practitioners and educational psychology researchers are concerned with measuring the outcomes of these interventions. The scientific approach in psychology is associated with quantifiable data. That is information that can be measured and presented as numbers. Below are some **quantitative** data collection methods commonly used in educational psychology research and evaluation.

> **Quantitative methods** Data collection and analysis that makes use of measurements and scores that are presented as numbers, summarised in tables and graph and analysed using statistical methods.

Standardised tests

Standardised tests are presented and scored according to detailed instructions. This method of data collection provides reliable scores that we can have confidence in. While some standardised tests are designed to provide an achievement score, others (often also referred to as norm-referenced tests) have tables of **standardised norms** that allow scores to be compared with other children of the same age. We saw some examples of these in

> **Standardised norms** Scales with norm-referenced data for comparison of individual's test performance with typical performance for children of the same age.

Chapter 1 with the Binet–Simon intelligence test (now updated as the Stanford-Binet Intelligence Scale). The Wechsler Intelligence Scale for Children is another commonly used standardised intelligence test. In Chapter 1, we also discussed the Burt Word Reading Test and Burt Word Spelling Test. Other examples of standardised reading tests are the Wechsler Individual Achievement Test and the Wide Range Achievement Test. Achenbach's Child Behaviour Checklist is an example of a frequently used norm-referenced scale completed by parents, teachers, or young people themselves to assess emotional and behavioural problems in children.

Surveys

Data may be gathered by questionnaire or interview from a group of participants. They will comprise self-report on attitudes, or behaviours or beliefs about a topic of interest, and the descriptive data collected can then be analysed together for the group. Parents of upper primary school children might be asked to take part in a **survey**, for example, on their preferences regarding their children's homework, quantity, level of challenge, and frequency. Analysis of the data collected would indicate to the school parents' opinions and help staff decide whether they would have parental support for increasing nightly homework expectations. Survey data can be further analysed to compare groups, for example, views of parents at school A on homework compared to parents at school B. Or the relationship between different variables can be examined, fathers' views compared to mothers' views.

Survey Questionnaire or interview using participants' self-reports to investigate a group's beliefs, opinions, attitudes, or behaviours regarding a particular topic.

Critical thinking task 7.1

You are a senior staff member in the upper primary school which comprises two classes of 30 children in each class. You have been given the responsibility of leading on homework policy. 16 mothers and 2

fathers completed the above survey. Analysis of data showed that parents feel that too much homework being sent home.
Are you satisfied that these findings are sound?
How would you take this forward?

Sociometric analysis

Children are interviewed individually and asked, for example, which three children they like to play with and which three children they don't like to play with. From this information, a diagram can be drawn of the social relationships in the class. This is a sociogram. In a **sociometric analysis**, children classified as 'popular' are those with a higher than median number of positive nominations and a lower than median number of negative nominations. Those scoring higher on negative nominations and lower on positive nominations are considered 'rejected'. Those scoring lower than median on both positive and negative nominations are categorised as 'isolated'. This peer nomination procedure is used to identify social status within the class and has been applied for example to study social inclusion of children with special needs and disabilities (Wilbert et al., 2020) or to investigate bullying (Cañas et al., 2022).

> **Sociometric analysis** A method for exploring friendships and popularity to help in understanding relationships and social structure within a group such as a school class.

Numerical data collected by the above methods can be summarised and organised visually into tables and graphs, which make understanding and interpretation easier. Educational psychology researchers typically want to know cause-and-effect. Did this intervention cause this outcome? By applying **inferential statistical** procedures, we can use data collected from the study sample to make inferences and generalisations beyond that study sample. We

> **Inferential statistics** Process by which generalisations about a population can be made from data drawn from a sample of that population.

can measure children's reading performance before and after a new reading programme and aim to determine from statistical analysis of the numerical data if the programme is effective. Is this a small before-and-after difference that has happened by chance or is it a significant difference that we should pay attention to? If the difference is statistically significant the researchers need to be confident that their findings do not just apply to the schools that they studied but can be generalised to other schools. A policy decision can then be made to roll out the successful programme to all the schools in the district. The use of inferential statistics to inform such decisions is too large and complex a topic to be dealt with here and is the subject of many excellent textbooks, for example, Field's (2024) book *Discovering statistics.*

Commonly used study designs in educational psychology research

So what study design do we need, to be sure that it was the reading programme that caused the positive outcome rather than idiosyncrasies of the teachers or the classes where the study took place. Ideally, we would want to try to control for other variables that might influence the findings, so that the study is measuring only the effects of the reading intervention, the specific variable of interest to us. Randomly allocating participants to intervention and comparison groups is the gold standard way of doing this to eliminate bias. However, in educational psychology research, the unit of study is typically a class and is already in place, allocated by the school, and beyond the control of the researcher. With this drawback in mind, let's now examine some typical methods of data gathering in educational psychology research and the extent to which inferences about the population in general can be made from the study design. That is to say, the extent to which we can be confident that study findings are robust and can be generalised and rolled out to other schools.

Online resource 7.1 Data collection: describing and making inferences

Daniel Storage (2019). Why study statistics in psychology? 17 June. Available at: www.youtube.com/watch?v=nQ_5ta7_jyE (Accessed: 28 February 2025).

Single-group pre-test post-test design

The **single-group pre-test–post-test** is a method that is frequently used in evaluation of educational programmes as it is convenient for an educator to carry out with their class without the support of a research team or additional funding. It allows measurement of change following a class or group intervention where all participants receive the same intervention. Pre-test measurements are taken before the intervention and the post-test measurements collected after the intervention programme is completed. This is a quantitative study as numerical data are gathered.

> **Single-group pre-test post-test** There is only one intervention group in this design and no comparison group. There is no control of possible confounding variables. Maturity and test effects are possible confounds in this design.

Critical thinking task 7.2

What are the limitations of the single-group pre-test post-test design?
If results show an improvement in the class post-test scores, can we conclude that the intervention is successful?
Can we recommend that other classes should implement it?

As there is only an intervention group and no comparison group, this design produces descriptive data and does not control for any confounding variables. Caution should be exercised in interpreting changes here as indications of a successful programme. **Maturation** is a possible confounding variable, in that children are developing and growing older, smarter, and more experienced and that this may explain the improved scores and not the intervention. The class might have shown improved scores on the measure

> **Maturation** Improved scores may be due to children growing older and smarter and not to the intervention itself.

without any intervention just because they have matured. In addition, **test effects** may also explain the outcome where participants just get better at taking the test. Maturation and testing though are controlled for where there is also a comparison group as in a quasi-experimental design as these effects would be exhibited across both groups equally.

Test effects Participants show improved scores post-test because they are better at taking the test the second time. Test practice has caused the improvement, not the intervention.

Quasi-experimental design

The **quasi-experimental** design is common in education where an intervention is often delivered at the school or class level. There cannot be experimental manipulation by randomly allocating individuals to intervention group or comparison group because children are not randomly allocated to schools or classes. They are already in pre-existing groups which cannot be changed for the purpose of a study. Extraneous variables cannot be controlled for in real-world, field research in school as readily as they can in a laboratory study.

Quasi-experimental Pre-existing groups; e.g., two classes are compared with one receiving the intervention and other not. Possible confounding variables are not controlled for in this design as they would be in an experimental design where participants are randomly allocated to intervention and comparison groups.

A research study might compare a class who received the intervention with another class who didn't. It appears 'as if' it is an experimental study as it has a comparison group and an intervention group, but importantly without random allocation the two groups might not be similar for comparison purposes. This design is referred to as a quasi-experimental design. 'Quasi' is Latin for 'as if'. It is also referred to as a non-randomised pre-post design.

Threats to internal validity

If the intervention group shows greater progress on the target variable than the comparison group who didn't receive the intervention, can we conclude the intervention was successful? Let us consider other possible explanations for this improvement, other than the intervention having caused it. In addition to identifying maturation and test effects as threats to the ability of the single-group pre-test–post-test design to draw conclusions about intervention effectiveness, Campbell and Stanley (1966) and Cook and Campbell (1979) identified a number of threats to the ability of quasi-experimental studies to draw conclusions of causality. **Threats to the internal validity** of the study include:

Threats to internal validity These are explanations for research findings other than that the intervention caused the changed outcomes and why we cannot be confident in drawing conclusions about intervention success.

Selection bias The intervention and the comparison group may have differed in other ways. If the group selected for the intervention was more able, this, and not the intervention, could explain their better scores.

Selection bias The group allocated to the intervention is different in some way from the comparison group, for example, slightly older, so this may be the reason for the intervention group's improved outcomes and not the intervention.

History Suppose Class A receives six sessions of an intervention designed to improve mental health and they show improved

History The meaning of this term in the context of threats to internal validity is that improved scores may be due to some other experience that the child or class has had and not to the intervention itself.

outcomes on a children's anxiety scale compared to Class B who did not receive the intervention. If we look at the history of what has occurred, we may find that as well as experiencing the intervention, Class A is also experiencing a highly skilled teacher who is committed to this intervention and is implementing it with great enthusiasm. Class B, the comparison group, has a jaded, bored teacher who is considering leaving the profession as soon as possible. Teacher effectiveness rather than intervention effectiveness could explain the outcome.

Regression to the mean This can be an issue when the group chosen for the intervention has particularly poor pre-intervention scores. For example, the poorest readers in the class have been targeted for a reading intervention programme. Their low pre-test scorers may show slightly improved post-test scores, not due to the intervention but due to a tendency for scores to drift away from the extreme towards the mean over time. For the same reason, high pre-test scorers may have slightly poorer post-test scores.

Regression to the mean The tendency of extreme scores to drift in the direction of an average score over time.

History and regression to the mean (as well as maturation and test effects already discussed) can also explain post-test improvement in the single-group pre-test post-test design (Marsden & Torgerson, 2012).

Critical thinking task 7.3

You are a member of the staff team in an early intervention programme in an area of disadvantage. A parenting programme to help parents support their children's language development is planned. You have been asked you to evaluate it.
How would you go about it?
What are the difficulties?

Single-case experimental design

A case here may be an individual child, or an individual class, or even a school. If we are carrying out a behavioural intervention with incentives to encourage a child to stay in their seat and not wander about the classroom disturbing others, a baseline measure of the target behaviour is taken during Phase A, a no-intervention phase. This must be an objective, observable measurement, for example, a count of how many times or how many minutes the child is out of their seat in the morning session before break. The intervention (Phase B) is then introduced to encourage the child stay seated, and after it, the same variable is measured again with hopefully reduced number of times out of seat if the intervention worked. The variable is measured for a third time after another no-intervention period (Phase A). This is often referred to as ABA design. Return to baseline measurement in the second Phase A suggests that it was the intervention that caused the reversal in the targeted behaviour. This process is repeated, with three manipulations (A-B, B-A, A-B) recommended to demonstrate that it was the intervention that caused Phase B improved behaviour. Each case acts as its own control. You might also see the **single-case experimental design** in the literature under other names such as n of 1, small n design, single-case design, or time series design. This design works well for identifying what works for individuals where there aren't enough numbers of similar individuals to implement an experimental comparison group design, for example, children with special needs and disabilities (Plavnick & Ferreri, 2013).

> **Single-case experimental design** Examples of a single-case are a child, an individual class, or a school. This design requires usually three repeated measurements of baseline and intervention phases to establish that the intervention is indeed the cause of the changed measurement.

Online resource 7.2 Single-case experimental design
Institute of Education Science (2023). What Works Clearing House single case design. 17 March. Available at: www.youtube.com/watch?v=EyysEstp63I (Accessed: 28 February 2025).

Summary

This chapter highlighted the importance of evidence-based educational psychology practice and the role of quantitative data in supporting this. We discussed quantitative research methods that are commonly used in the naturalistic setting of a school or classroom and identified some challenges to being able to draw firm conclusions about the effects of intervention. Caution therefore needs to be exercised before taking forward any apparent findings to inform wider practice or policy.

References/Further reading

Campbell, D. T., & Stanley, J. C. (1966). *Experimental and quasi-experimental designs for research.* Houghton Mifflin.

Cañas, E., Estevez, E., & Estevez, J. F. (2022). Sociometric status in bullying perpetrators: A systematic review. *Frontiers in Communication*, *7*, 841424.

Clements, T., & Harding, E. (2023). Addressing the withdrawal of playtime: A collaborative action research project. *Educational Psychology in Practice*, *39*(3), 257–272. https://doi.org/10.1080/02667363.2023.2194610

Cook, T. D., & Campbell, D. T. (1979). *Quasi-experimentation: Design & analysis issues for field settings.* Houghton Mifflin.

Field, A. (2024). *Discovering statistics using IBM SPSS statistics.* Sage.

Frederickson, N. (2002). Evidence-based practice and educational psychology. *Educational and Child Psychology.*

Kratochwill, T. R. (2007). Preparing psychologists for evidence-based school practice: Lessons learned and challenges ahead. *American Psychologist*, *62*(8), 829.

Lilienfeld, S. O., Ammirati, R., & David, M. (2012). Distinguishing science from pseudoscience in school psychology: Science and scientific thinking as safeguards against human error. *Journal of School Psychology*, *50*(1), 7–36. https://doi.org/10.1016/j.jsp.2011.09.006

Marsden, E., & Torgerson, C. J. (2012). Single group, pre-and post-test research designs: Some methodological concerns. *Oxford Review of Education*, *38*(5), 583–616.

Plavnick, J. B., & Ferreri, S. J. (2013). Single-case experimental designs in educational research: A methodology for causal analyses in teaching and learning. *Educational Psychology Review*, *25*(4), 549–569. https://doi.org/10.1007/s10648-013-9230-6

Webster-Stratton, C., Rinaldi, J., & Reid, J. M. (2011). Long-term outcomes of Incredible Years Parenting Program: Predictors of adolescent adjustment. *Child and Adolescent Mental Health*, *16*(1), 38–46.

Wilbert, J., Urton, K., Krull, J., Kulawiak, P. R., Schwalbe, A., & Hennemann, T. (2020). Teachers' accuracy in estimating social inclusion of students with and without special educational needs. *Frontiers in Education*, *5*, 598330.

Chapter 8

Qualitative methods and mixed quantitative–qualitative methods in educational psychology

In Chapter 7, we examined the use of quantitative research in educational psychology and the challenges of carrying it out in the real-world setting of the classroom. The current chapter complements Chapter 7 by exploring the use of qualitative methodologies in educational psychology. Following the lead of the wider psychology discipline in viewing itself as a science, quantitative studies have been highly valued within educational psychology as a reliable source of scientific evidence, qualitative research less so. Prestigious educational psychology journals published only a very small number of qualitative research papers. This has, however, gradually increased in recent years as educational psychology researchers became more aware of how qualitative research illuminates understanding and also importantly how to ensure trustworthiness of findings by delivering rigour in this work that parallels the rigour of quantitative research (Sabnis et al., 2023; Sabnis & Wolgemuth, 2024). We will consider criteria for rigour in qualitative data collection and analysis and then go on to discuss mixed methods research, the use of quantitative and qualitative data collection and analysis within the same study.

Qualitative researchers collect rich, in-depth, descriptive data. Rather than examining specific variables under controlled conditions, their interest is in individuals' experiences within the messy real-world situations they

Qualitative methods Collection of rich, in-depth, data from individuals or groups describing their thoughts and actions in messy, real-world situations.

DOI: 10.4324/9781032691541-11

inhabit. While the currency of **quantitative** research is numbers, for qualitative research it is words. Analysis for qualitative research then is verbal rather than statistical. Qualitative methods recognise and address subjectivity, while quantitative methods value objectivity. New theory and understandings can emerge from analysis of qualitative data, while quantitative methods test out explicitly stated hypotheses (Bryman, 2016; Denzin et al., 2023; Hammersley, 2012; Howitt & Cramer, 2010).

Quantitative methods Data collection and analysis that makes use of measurements and scores that are presented as numbers, summarised in tables and graph and analysed using statistical methods.

Online resource 8.1 Qualitative research
Office of Research and Doctoral Services (2015). Overview of qualitative research methods. 13 August. Available at: www.youtube.com/watch?v=IsAUNs-IoSQ (Accessed: 28 February 2025).

Interviews

A common method of gathering qualitative information is the **interview**. This can be individual interviews or **focus groups** where interviews are carried out in small groups. Interviews can be unstructured, semi-structured, or structured. Structured interviews are useful in large projects with multiple interviewers as it allows some standardisation across interviewers, but there is no flexibility to explain or elaborate on the questions. Unstructured interviews are more conversational with the researcher having identified topics of interest to the study but otherwise leaving the direction of the interview open. Interviews should largely be one-sided with the interviewee doing most of the talking and just key prompts from the interviewer (Gullion,

Focus group A small group of people who are similar in some way, for example, parents or teachers, who are chosen to discuss a topic relevant to them.

2024). Sabnis and Wolgemuth (2024) found semi-structured interviews to be the most common form of qualitative data collection in educational psychology, followed by focus groups. Semi-structured interviews use some key questions with flexibility to follow up with new questions areas of interest that emerge through the interview process.

Focus groups typically involve around six to ten participants discussing as a group, questions, or a topic, or perhaps curriculum materials, provided by the researcher. Nind et al. (2022) propose focus groups as a particularly valuable method for inclusive research where instead of carrying out research 'on' people and using them as sources of information, the interactive space of a focus group facilitates carrying out research 'with' people. This can be a beneficial setting for participants who can learn more about themselves and the situation under discussion from each other's contributions to the group.

Some examples of qualitative studies in education using interviews:

- Teachers' views of assessment where semi-structured interviews were carried out with 30 primary and 20 secondary teachers (Remesal, 2011).
- Semi-structured interviews with 21 elementary school teachers on providing support to traumatised children (Alisic, 2012).
- Two focus groups with 13 parents of children with attention deficit hyperactivity disorder (ADHD) to investigate their experience of stress (Leitch et al., 2019).

Critical thinking task 8.1

Consider in what circumstances you might use a focus group and when individual interviews might be more useful?
What criteria would you use to inform your decision?

Classroom observation

An important qualitative method for understanding how teaching and learning take place in a classroom is *in situ* observation. **Classroom observation** can be used in research studies; or by practitioner educational psychologists in their casework, observing an individual child referred to psychological services for behaviour problems; or by teachers carrying out peer-review, observing each other's teaching for professional development and to improve standards. Observation may be carried out naturalistically taking notes on what is observed or using some degree of structure in order to focus the observer's attention. In lab-based studies, the observer can watch the interaction for example between mothers and children through a one-way mirror as in Jones' (2007) study of infants imitating their mothers' actions. For classroom observations, the observer is usually in a classroom with the students and teacher. Their role may be as a 'pure' observer from outside the class or as a participant observer who has a relationship with the class or teacher being studied (Robson, 2024). A practitioner educational psychologist sits somewhere along this continuum. If they have worked often with the class teacher on a range of issues as well as with many of the students in the class, they might be considered more of a participant observer than say a researcher from the local university.

Classroom observation can be quantitative when numerical data are collected. For example, Apter et al.'s (2020) on teacher feedback recruited 33 educational psychologists to act as observers in 28 secondary schools. They categorised teacher feedback comments as positive or critical about an academic task or about social behaviour. Psychologist-observers also counted the amount of teacher talk in the lesson and whether it was instruction, explanation, or exposition. In this case, the researchers examined relationships between teacher feedback and student on-task behaviour using inferential statistics.

Document analysis

Document analysis Systematic analysis of written documents such as anti-bullying policy and teacher lesson plans.

Written documents are examined, for example, school policy documents, teacher lesson plans, and their contents analysed systematically for themes of interest. These may be documents that were written for a different purpose prior to the study or documents written to be analysed in the study. Calderón et al. (2024) examined pre-service teachers' lesson planning documents and their written reflections to explore how their online learning had transferred to their classroom practice. Sievert et al. (2021) studied the content of mathematics textbooks to determine the extent to which they facilitated early years transition from counting using concrete measures for addition and subtraction to calculating or memorising the answer. It should be noted, as in Sievert et al.'s study, that document analysis often also makes use of quantitative measures.

The distinguishing feature of good qualitative research is that data collection and analysis is rigorous, systematic, and transparent. Anecdotal description of an anti-bullying intervention is considered less rigorous than research where researchers document how they carried out thematic analysis and used inter-rater checks on coding of the interview transcript data into these themes. If we are trying to answer a question about what works, we need to assess qualitative research findings to decide the extent to which we can have confidence that the results reported can be generalised to our own setting, just as for quantitative results. We need to be aware of the researcher's own values and biases. Is the study an evaluation of a mental health programme for secondary school students where the researcher was also the programme developer? Reading a report of positive intervention findings, we'd certainly want to know if this is the case.

Criteria for evaluating qualitative research

Confirmability

This criterion relates to the idea of objectivity and that the findings are not simply subjective and a reflection of the researcher's own biases. A detailed audit trail reporting each stage of data collection and analysis aids **confirmability**, demonstrating a clear link between the method and findings reported.

Confirmability Criterion for evaluating trustworthiness of qualitative research that parallels the criterion of objectivity in quantitative research.

Dependability

Has the study been designed and carried out with care? Are the research questions and design clearly specified and consistent with each other? Is the researcher's role made explicit? Were coding checks made to eliminate biased coding? Could the research process be replicated by other investigators and still deliver the same findings? **Dependability** parallels the idea of reliability in quantitative research.

Dependability Criterion for evaluating trustworthiness of qualitative research that parallels reliability in quantitative research.

Credibility

Do the conclusions seem credible and truthful to study participants and to those reading the study report? Miles et al. (2019) considered this the key question about the value of a qualitative study. Rich descriptions and quotes facilitate readers' decisions about the meaningfulness and authenticity of the findings. Member checks can also enhance **credibility**. This is where interview data are checked with participants and confirmed or modified. This can be checking of the interview transcript, or of interpreted data such as coding of an individual participant's interview, or of emerging themes identified from the study as a whole (Birt et al., 2016). It is similar to the concept of internal validity in quantitative research.

Credibility Criterion for evaluating trustworthiness of qualitative research that parallels internal validity in quantitative research.

Transferability

The issue here is whether these conclusions have wider applicability and can transfer to another class or school or do they only apply to this class and these participants. **Transferability** is similar to the concepts of generalisability and

Transferability Criterion for evaluating trustworthiness of qualitative research that parallels generalisability and external validity in quantitative research.

external validity in quantitative research (Denzin et al., 2023; Miles et al., 2019).

Online resource 8.2 Trustworthiness in qualitative research
Jenny Barrow (2019). Trustworthiness in qualitative research. 12 July. Available at: www.youtube.com/watch?v=V66KYGCq0IM (Accessed: 28 February 2025).

Mixed methods research

Quantitative and qualitative methods take very different philosophical approaches to gathering information. Quantitative methods are underpinned by the idea that there is an external, objective reality that can be measured. Qualitative methods on the other hand are underpinned by **social constructivism** that individuals construct their own interpretation of reality within a social context. Gage (1989) referred to these competing research principles as 'paradigm wars' and noted that eventually there grew a realisation that there was not only one true paradigm and that difference did not need to mean conflict. Wittrock (1992) proposed that applying both quantitative and qualitative methods of research was the way forward for educational psychology. The complexity of the social and cultural contexts in which educational psychology research is carried out where classes are embedded in schools with their own distinctive cultures points to the need for **mixed methods research** (Nolen, 2020). This is an evolving field which can involve collecting and analysing both quantitative and qualitative data separately within a single study or can involve a

Social constructivism Individuals construct their own understanding of the world through interaction with the social and cultural context of their environment.

Mixed methods research Research study that applies both quantitative and qualitative methods for a more in-depth understanding of a topic of interest.

greater degree of synthesis and integration of the findings of the two types of data (Tashakkori & Creswell, 2007).

Online resource 8.3 What is mixed methods research?
Michigan Medicine (2023). What is mixed methods research? 12 January. Available at: www.youtube.com/watch?v=II_OoioL0-E (Accessed: 28 February 2025).

There are different purposes in carrying out mixed methods research (Caracelli & Greene, 1993; Greene et al., 1989):

Triangulation The process of convergence and corroboration of concurrent qualitative and quantitative data sources for confirmation of findings with equal status given to each.

Complementarity Different or overlapping aspects or different levels of the phenomenon under study are investigated using qualitative and quantitative methods. This enables elaboration of one method's results with the other and helps with complexity.

Development Results of one method are sequentially used to inform or develop the other method. There is dynamic interplay of methods here.

Initiation This is the provocative use of qualitative and quantitative methods to look for new insights by searching for contradictions between them.

Expansion This purpose expands the range of the study by using different methods for different elements of the research. One method expands the findings of the other either sequentially or concurrently, and not necessarily equal in priority.

Critical thinking task 8.2

Reflecting on Critical thinking task 7.3 where you were asked to evaluate a parenting programme, what value might adding a qualitative dimension contribute to this investigation?

Box 8.1 Case study: mixed methods research on the effects of an online intervention with secondary students

Donohoe et al. (2012) were interested in investigating non-academic factors that impact on school achievement. Dweck's growth mindset theory is one such factor, focused on learners' beliefs that their abilities and skills can be developed (Dweck, 2017). The research team carried out an exploratory small-scale mixed methods study to try to better understand this complex issue. The Brainology programme was devised by Dweck to be delivered online to encourage a growth mindset through activities that promote the idea to participants that effort and learning strategies will improve how their brains work when engaged in their school studies.

The quantitative study was a **quasi-experimental** design with intervention and comparison groups who were not randomly selected. The qualitative study was sequential to the quantitative study with semi-structured questions informed by the quantitative findings. Both sets of data were integrated in the discussion.

Quasi-experimental Pre-existing groups; e.g., two classes are compared with one receiving the intervention and other not. Possible confounding variables are not controlled for in this design as they would be in an experimental design where participants are randomly allocated to intervention and comparison groups.

Thirty-three pupils in a Scottish secondary school participated in the study, 18 in the intervention group and 15 in the comparison group. Quantitative measures utilised a scale that measured growth mindset by examining students' implicit theories of intelligence and a scale that measured resiliency. This was followed by focus group discussions. Both quantitative and qualitative data indicated intervention group students moving towards growth mindsets. The researchers reported that the qualitative data added new insights on social context and peer perceptions into the existing body of quantitative evidence about the development of growth mindsets.

Donohoe, C., Topping, K., & Hannah, E. (2012). The impact of an online intervention (Brainology) on the mindset and resiliency of secondary school pupils: a preliminary mixed methods study. *Educational Psychology, 32*, 641–655.

Summary

In this chapter, we explored some commonly used qualitative methods in the field of educational psychology and criterion to ensure their trustworthiness. We also recognised how mixing qualitative and quantitative methods in a study can add to our depth of understanding of a research topic.

References/Further reading

Alisic, E. (2012). Teachers' perspectives on providing support to children after trauma: A qualitative study. *School Psychology Quarterly*, *27*(1), 51.

Apter, B., Sulla, F., & Swinson, J. (2020). A review of recent large-scale systematic UK classroom observations, method and findings, utility and impact. *Educational Psychology in Practice*, *36*(4), 367–385. https://doi.org/10.1080/02667363.2020.1802233

Birt, L., Scott, S., Cavers, D., Campbell, C., & Walter, F. (2016). Member checking: A tool to enhance trustworthiness or merely a nod to validation? *Qualitative Health Research*, *26*(13), 1802–1811. https://doi.org/10.1177/1049732316654870

Bryman, A. (2016). *Social research methods.* Oxford University Press.

Calderón, A., Masterson, M., & Boynuegri, E. (2024). Learning online and teaching face to face: Exploring the planned and enacted conception of teaching of preservice teachers on school placement. *Teaching and Teacher Education*, *144*, 104598. https://doi.org/https://doi.org/10.1016/j.tate.2024.104598

Caracelli, V. J., & Greene, J. C. (1993). Data analysis strategies for mixed-method evaluation designs. *Educational Evaluation and Policy Analysis, 15*(2), 195–207.

Denzin, N. K., Lincoln, Y. S., Giardina, M. D., & Cannella, G. S. (2023). *The Sage handbook of qualitative research.* Sage publications.

Donohoe, C., Topping, K., & Hannah, E. (2012). The impact of an online intervention (Brainology) on the mindset and resiliency of secondary school pupils: A preliminary mixed methods study. *Educational Psychology, 32*(5), 641–655. https://doi.org/10.1080/01443410.2012.675646

Dweck, C. S. (2017). The journey to children's mindsets—and beyond. *Child Development Perspectives, 11*(2), 139–144. https://doi.org/https://doi.org/10.1111/cdep.12225

Gage, N. (1989). The paradigm wars and their aftermath. A "historical" sketch of research on teaching since 1989. *Educational Researcher, 18*(7), 4–10. https://doi.org/10.3102/0013189x018007004

Greene, J. C., Caracelli, V. J., & Graham, W. F. (1989). Toward a conceptual framework for mixed-method evaluation designs. *Educational Evaluation and Policy Analysis, 11*(3), 255–274. https://doi.org/10.3102/01623737011003255

Gullion, J. S. (2024). Qualitative research in health and illness. Oxford University Press. https://doi.org/10.1093/oso/9780190915988.003.0006

Hammersley, M. (2012). *What is qualitative research?* Bloomsbury Academic.

Howitt, D., & Cramer, D. (2010). *Introduction to qualitative methods in psychology.* Pearson Education.

Jones, S. S. (2007). Imitation in infancy: The development of mimicry. *Psychological Science, 18*(7), 593–599.

Leitch, S., Sciberras, E., Post, B., Gerner, B., Rinehart, N., Nicholson, J. M., & Evans, S. (2019). Experience of stress in parents of children with ADHD: A qualitative study. *International Journal of Qualitative Studies on Health and Well-Being, 14*(1), 1690091.

Miles, M., Huberman, M., & Saldaňa, J. (2019). *Qualitative data analysis: A methods sourcebook* (Fourth ed.). Sage.

Nind, M., Kaley, A., & Hall, E. (2022). Focus group method. In P. Liamputtong (Ed.), *Handbook of social inclusion: Research and practices in health and social sciences* (pp. 1041–1061). Springer International Publishing. https://doi.org/10.1007/978-3-030-89594-5_57

Nolen, S. B. (2020). Challenging research norms in educational psychology. *Educational Psychologist, 55*(4), 267–272. https://doi.org/10.1080/00461520.2020.1810043

Remesal, A. (2011). Primary and secondary teachers' conceptions of assessment: A qualitative study. *Teaching and Teacher Education*, *27*(2), 472–482. https://doi.org/https://doi.org/10.1016/j.tate.2010.09.017

Robson, C. (2024). *Real world research* (Fifth ed.). John Wiley & Sons.

Sabnis, S. V., Newman, D. S., Whitford, D., & Mossing, K. (2023). Publication and characteristics of qualitative research in School Psychology journals between 2006 and 2021. *School Psychology*, *38*(5), 330.

Sabnis, S. V., & Wolgemuth, J. R. (2024). Common misconceptions and good practices in qualitative research in school psychology. *Journal of School Psychology*, *106*, 101328. https://doi.org/https://doi.org/10.1016/j.jsp.2024.101328

Sievert, H., van den Ham, A.-K., & Heinze, A. (2021). Are first graders' arithmetic skills related to the quality of mathematics textbooks? A study on students' use of arithmetic principles. *Learning and Instruction*, *71*, 101401. https://doi.org/https://doi.org/10.1016/j.learninstruc.2020.101401

Tashakkori, A., & Creswell, J. W. (2007). Editorial: The new era of mixed methods. *Journal of Mixed Methods Research*, *1*(1), 3–7. https://doi.org/10.1177/2345678906293042

Wittrock, M. C. (1992). An empowering conception of educational psychology. *Educational Psychologist*, *27*(2), 129–141. https://doi.org/10.1207/s15326985ep2702_1

Chapter 9

How to examine research findings on interventions critically

We started the process of examining research findings critically in Chapters 7 and 8. We considered threats to the internal validity of quantitative research designs commonly used in educational research, that is, to say threats to how confident we could be that the findings show that the intervention caused the outcome, rather than that it might be caused by other variables that the study hadn't controlled for. We similarly examined parameters of trustworthiness in qualitative research with the intention that these understandings are applied when evaluating research findings. In this chapter, we add some complementary ideas. We will clarify why correlations should not be interpreted as causation. We distinguish efficacy from effectiveness, and clinical significance from statistical significance. The chapter introduces the newer field of implementation science. Finally, it shows how consideration of the hierarchy of research designs can help us have confidence in study findings and indicate some sources of user-friendly syntheses of research findings for educators to aid decisions about interventions.

Correlation is not causation

Correlational research is a good example of data that are manageable for a **practitioner educational psychologist** or teacher gathering information

Practitioner/professional educational psychologist School psychologist carries out applied work with children, school staff, carers, and families. This might be at the level of the individual child, the family, the classroom, the school, or the school district.

DOI: 10.4324/9781032691541-12

about their own work with a class. At its simplest level, the educator can administer two questionnaires or tests to a class at a single session and examine the statistical relationship between them. Some examples of correlational studies:

Kidwai and Smith (2024) reported a small negative relationship between the range of coverage of school anti-bullying policies and students' self-reports of experience of bullying. A negative **correlation** means that while one variable increases, the other decreases. In this case, where the content of the school's anti-bullying policy increased, student reports of being bullied decreased.

Correlation A consistent relationship between two variables such that they change together.

Corthorn and Milicic (2016) found a significant negative correlation between mindfulness in parents and depression, anxiety, and parenting stress.

Pinquart and Ebeling (2020) found a positive association (correlation) between parental expectations and child achievement.

Correlational studies are useful in providing preliminary data that allow us to identify patterns and develop new insights that lead to explanatory theories about why these measures might be associated. Thinking back to **threats to internal validity** in Chapter 7, the extent to which we can be sure that there is a causal relationship, you can see that in a correlation study there is no attempt to control any confounding variables. This means that there may be a third confounding variable in a correlation study that we are not aware of and did not control for. In educational psychology, we are primarily interested in what a finding

Threats to internal validity Explanations for research findings other than that the intervention caused the changed outcomes and why we cannot be confident in drawing conclusions about intervention success.

might mean for improving learning or wellbeing or behaviour or teaching. What can we conclude from a correlation finding?

Let's think about this. Consider an educational psychology study that shows an association between the number of computers in a school and children's reading achievement. Can we conclude that putting more computers in classrooms will cause increased reading achievement?

The answer is no, because correlation does not mean **causation.** Firstly, a correlational relationship does not have a direction, so while we can say the number of computers is correlated with reading achievement, we could equally say reading achievement is correlated with the number of computers. While we might seriously wonder if increasing computers would increase reading achievement, would you think as seriously about the other way of expressing the relationship that improved children's reading scores will cause the number of computers to increase? Of course not. There is no sensible theory that could explain why the relationship between the two variables might occur in this direction. We would need a third variable here, for example, that the school parent association buys more computers because they are happy with their children's progress in reading and want to support the school both by helping with their children's reading and buying equipment. So, the relationship found between number of computers and reading achievement might be explained by a confounding variable that was not measured in the study such as parental support or the school being in an affluent area which influences both the number of computers and also the number of books in school and at home.

Causation The relationship between two events where one event, for example, an intervention programme, influences or causes a change in an event that follows, for example, a change in measured outcomes.

Online resource 9.1 Correlation is not causation

DATAtab (2023). Causality (and the difference to correlation) simply explained. 24 July. Available at: www.youtube.com/watch?v=IeyQvFhFyiY (Accessed: 28 February 2025).

Critical thinking task 9.1

For each of the correlational relationships below consider whether there is a third variable that might explain the association.

1 *Child's age and child's shoe size.*
2 *Parent participation in Incredible Years Parent Training programme and improved child behaviour.*
3 *Time spent on maths homework and performance in class maths test.*
4 *School anti-bullying policy document and reduction in bullying behaviours.*
5 *School anti-bullying programme and reduction in bullying behaviours.*
6 *School breakfast club and improved child completion of work tasks during class.*

Efficacy or effectiveness?

Let's address now the distinction between the terms '**effectiveness**' and '**efficacy**'. They are not interchangeable. Throughout these last chapters, we have wrestled with the limitations on drawing firm conclusions about causality in the real-life educational psychology setting of the school because of inability to control for possible confounding variables. This is an effectiveness study where we evaluate the outcome of an intervention in a naturalistic setting with pre-existing groups. The drawback here is lack of control but there is also an advantage, ecological validity, because there are no attempts to manipulate variables, so the context measured is completely realistic.

Effectiveness The outcome of an intervention is evaluated in a real-world setting.

Efficacy Intervention study is carried out under ideal conditions controlling for confounding variables, including random allocation of participants into intervention groups and comparison groups.

Efficacy research aims to test out the hypothesis under ideal conditions and so will control confounding variables as far as possible. An efficacy study will randomly allocate participants into intervention groups and comparison groups. There will be inclusion and exclusion criteria for participation in the study. However, if we want to take the results of a successful efficacy study forward into a real-world setting, an effectiveness study would need to be carried out.

A related value that we should also consider in applying rigorous efficacy findings to real-life settings is whether the intended users of the research consider the intervention acceptable to them and whether it is cost-effective. That is to say we need to take into account whether this intervention is 'efficient' (Dunst & Trivette, 2012; Marley, 2000). We may design an excellent study, controlling for confounding variables and obtaining the results we hope for, but if, for example, the programme requires parents to engage in reading activities with their children for two hours per day, it will probably not be implemented consistently. Parents may not want to commit to doing this, or if they did commit, they would probably not be able to sustain it. And if they have two children, or three or more? Parents may not view this as a reasonable or efficient use of their time and resources, even though a research study had shown the programme to be successful.

Statistical significance versus clinical significance

When appropriate statistical tests are carried out on measurement data, the analysis shows whether the results obtained could be due to chance or whether the probability (p) of that is very small, less than .5, so we can be confident that we have a significant difference, say, between an intervention group and a comparison group or between pre- and post-intervention. The difference can be very small though, so although a study is statistically significant, it may not be sufficiently clinically significant to make it worth the time and effort for education staff or parents to deliver the intervention or for participants to take part in the programme.

Clinical significance in educational psychology is about how large the change is and whether it matters, the impact of the change to the child or to others with whom the child interacts (peers, family, education staff), how long the effects last, and acceptability to participants and those delivering the intervention, cost-effectiveness, and ease of implementation (Kazdin, 1999; Ranganathan et al., 2015). You can see there are some commonalities between the concepts of clinical significance and efficiency and barriers studied in implementation science below.

Clinical significance This is about whether change resulting from an intervention is of practical significance, whether it matters to intervention participants in the real-world setting.

Online resource 9.2 Clinical significance and statistical significance

Rich Simpson (2020). Statistical v clinical significance. 3 August. Available at: www.youtube.com/watch?v=E7934CSKkN4 (Accessed: 28 February 2025).

Box 9.1 Case study: Is this statistically significant numeracy intervention worth it?

Ms James who we met in Chapter 4 is known to be particularly interested in the teaching of mathematics in the primary school where she works. The head teacher, Mrs Patel, is concerned about children experiencing, or at risk of experiencing, difficulties in basic arithmetic. In discussion with an educational psychologist, Mrs Patel wants to implement a programme in small groups with 6–8-year-olds who are struggling. Ms James is asked to lead this intervention project with the small groups, and a temporary teacher is brought in to cover Ms James class when she is doing this. She works with five groups of six children on 15 min daily sessions for 20 weeks. Each group receives intensive practice with number bonds with the aim of reducing their reliance on counting on their fingers. The educational psychologist identified children in other schools who receive their usual maths teaching (teaching-as-usual) to form a comparison group and carried out pre- and post-evaluations.

At the end of 20 weeks, the educational psychologist reported a statistically significant difference between the intervention and comparison group of 3 points.

Mrs Patel discussed this with Ms James and the management team. While she was pleased that the intervention was found to be successful, she needed to decide if it was worth repeating. The team discussed how meaningful a 3-point difference is when the overall scores were still quite low. Would the intervention group show a noticeable improvement in their number bond work in class? The team discussed resourcing issues such as whether this was best use of Ms James' time and the additional expense of the extra teacher to cover Ms James' class. After much deliberation, Mrs Patel decided that effects of this intervention were not sufficient to outweigh resourcing costs and that such intensity of input was not sustainable in the longer term for the school.

Although statistically significant, the outcome was not viewed as clinically significant.

Implementation science

Suppose a wellbeing programme designed to help young people cope with anxiety requires a teacher to deliver an evidence-based, manualised set of lessons once a week for six weeks as part of the timetabled subject *Relationships and Health Education*. The programme has already been shown to be successful in both efficacy and effectiveness research studies. The teacher who received training on the programme, however, only managed to deliver four sessions due to absence. Another teacher who was not trained in the programme covered the two remaining sessions, not from the manual but using a self-devised lesson plan. Because of these changes and lack of consistency, **programme fidelity** was not maintained, and the class did not receive the rigorously evaluated, evidence-based programme, but instead received a weaker hybrid, which was not supported by research evidence, and may not result in the expected outcomes in improved coping with anxiety.

Programme fidelity The extent to which an intervention is implemented as intended and how faithful the actual programme delivery is to its original plan.

The gap between a research study carried out under controlled conditions and routine implementation in schools or at home is a significant one and worthy of study in itself as higher levels of implementation lead to better outcomes. To study this, we must systematically study implementation failure. We need to examine barriers in the process of translating research findings to the real-world context of everyday applied professional practice. We need to study how to improve the relationship between evidence-based practice findings and practitioner behaviour. This new area of study for educational psychology is known as **implementation science** (Forman et al., 2013; Kelly, 2013; Moir, 2018). We will return to this in Chapter 12.

Implementation science Systematic study of barriers and facilitators in order to improve the uptake of evidence-based research findings into practice.

Critical thinking task 9.2

The Olweus Bullying Prevention Programme https://clemsonolweus.org/ has a robust evidence base and has been used internationally. Silverton Primary School has decided to deliver this programme to Years 5 and 6.

What are the possible barriers to implementation and what can the school do to avoid or overcome these?

Hierarchy of research designs

Chapters 7, 8, and 9 all advocate the importance of evidence-based practice in educational psychology. A **hierarchy of**

evidence helps us in the task of appraising evidence by providing an overarching ranking of the different sources of evidence discussed in these chapters. This ranking of research designs reflects decreasing **threats to internal validity** (see Chapter 7) as we move upwards. In 2005, the American Psychological Association (APA) Presidential Task Force made a statement on how to evaluate research evidence on which to base professional practice. The APA located clinical opinion at the bottom of this hierarchy, followed by systematic observation, and then sophisticated research methodologies which included **quasi-experimental** designs and **randomised controlled** experiments. They viewed randomised controlled experimental trials (RCTs) as being at the top of the hierarchy of designs for minimising threats to internal validity (APA, 2006). In an RCT, participants are allocated to intervention and comparison groups by a random chance process. This process is assumed to control for possible confounding variables equally across both groups so that group differences found after the intervention can be considered as due to the intervention itself.

Hierarchy of evidence This is a ranking of research designs that reflects decreasing threats to internal validity.

Quasi-experimental Pre-existing groups; e.g., two classes are compared with one receiving the intervention and other not. Possible confounding variables are not controlled for in this design as they would be in an experimental design where participants are randomly allocated to intervention and comparison groups.

Randomised controlled trial (RCT) Gold standard experimental design. Participants are allocated to intervention and comparison groups by a random chance process. This process is assumed to control for possible confounding variables equally across both groups so that group differences found after the intervention can be considered as due to the intervention itself.

APA's updated policy on evidence-based practice in psychology (APA, 2021) makes use of a three-part model that advocates integration of the best research as in the hierarchy of evidence, along with practitioner expertise, and client preferences.

The National Institute for Clinical Excellence (NICE) has similar guidelines updated in 2023 with RCTs at the top of the hierarchy but recognising that RCTs are not always ethical or appropriate or possible and that non-randomised studies will be the best source of evidence. As discussed in Chapter 7, this is often the case in educational psychology research where we are working with classes or groups that are pre-existing and re-allocation for the purposes of a research study is not possible. NICE places qualitative research and expert opinion lower in the hierarchy and views these as useful for supplementing experimental sources of data.

The above evidence guidelines have been developed for healthcare professionals working in clinical settings and are also useful for those working in educational psychology, but additionally there are also education-specific resources for evaluating research.

The Evidence for Policy and Practice Information (EPPI) Centre at University College London Institute of Education conducts **systematic reviews** where the results from several studies are synthesised. The EPPI centre works at the cutting edge of systematic review methodology, developing methods and training researchers. It produces user-friendly syntheses of research findings for teachers, parents, and policymakers to help them decide whether the scientific evidence for an intervention indicates that it is worth delivering. **Meta-analysis** is another method of synthesising multiple findings. It is a statistical method of systematically integrating results from similar datasets from many studies on the same

Systematic review Results from several studies on the same question are synthesised. Meta-analysis may be included as part of a systematic review.

Meta-analysis Statistical method of systematically synthesising similar datasets from many studies on the same research question.

research question. When carried out rigorously, expertly, and when statistical anomalies are addressed, systematic reviews and meta-analyses are considered optimal sources of evidence.

Online resource 9.3 What is the difference between a systematic review and a meta-analysis?
University of South Australia (2022). The difference between systematic review and meta-analysis. 18 August Available at: www.youtube.com/watch?v=2q5ckDTmP2M&t=158s (Accessed: 28 February 2025).

What Works Clearinghouse (WWC) is the research branch of the United States Department of Education, and it provides excellent information for people working in education who want to use best evidence for deciding on whether to implement an intervention. They can search WWC webpages to find the education intervention they are thinking of and read WWC's evaluation of the extent to which the evidence has a sound scientific basis. WWC classifies evidence as strong, moderate, or minimal. Strong category meets WWC standards without reservations, for example, a well-designed RCT without participant dropout.

Online resource 9.4 How WWC evaluates studies
WWC resources (2021). WWC study ratings. 22 February Available at: https://ies.ed.gov/ncee/WWC/Resources/Evidence (Accessed: 28 February 2025).

The Campbell Collaboration also covers research in education and provides accessible research syntheses from systematic reviews and meta-analyses to aid decision-making.

Online resource 9.5 Campbell Collaboration systematic reviews
The Campbell Collaboration (2010). What is evidence-based practice? Aron Shlonsky. 29 June. Available at: www.youtube.com/watch?v=HcHg511DNFc (Accessed: 28 February 2025).

We have seen that in order to critically evaluate research findings to identify evidence-based interventions, medicine, health, and education have all developed similar hierarchies of research evidence. You will often see this presented as a pyramid, an example of which is below.

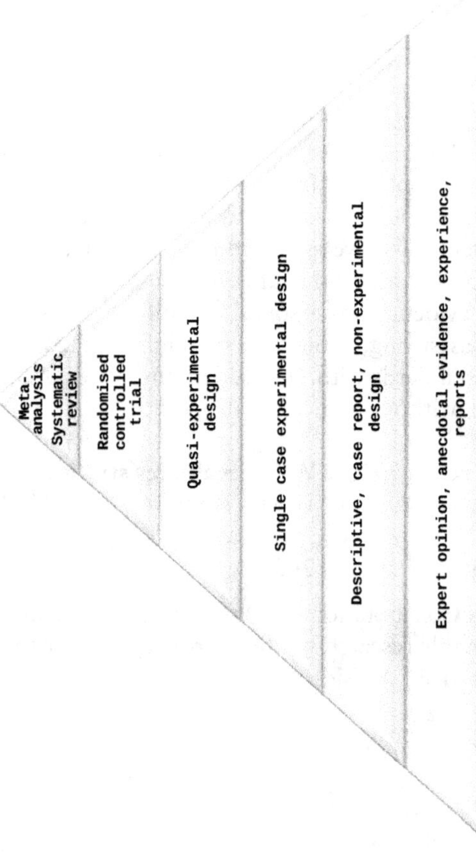

Figure 9.1 Evidence hierarchy pyramid.

Summary

In this chapter, we continued our critical appraisal of key methodologies in educational psychology intervention evaluation. We recognised how these can be ranked to increase our confidence in the findings reported. Various helpful sources of synthesised findings for education interventions were identified here.

References/Further reading

APA (2006). Evidence-based practice in psychology. APA Presidential Task Force on evidence-based practice. *American Psychologist*, *61*, 271–285. https://doi.org/doi:10.1037/0003–066X.61.4.271.

APA (2021). *Professional practice guidelines for evidence-based psychological practice in health care*. www.apa.org/about/policy/evidence-based-psychological-practice-health-care.pdf

Corthorn, C., & Milicic, N. (2016). Mindfulness and parenting: A correlational study of non-meditating mothers of preschool children. *Journal of Child and Family Studies*, *25*, 1672–1683.

Dunst, C. J., & Trivette, C. M. (2012). Meta-analysis of implementation practice research. In B. Kelly & D. Perkins (Eds.), *Handbook of implementation science for psychology in education* (pp. 68–91). Cambridge University Press.

Forman, S. G., Shapiro, E. S., Codding, R. S., Gonzales, J. E., Reddy, L. A., Rosenfield, S. A. … Stoiber, K. C. (2013). Implementation science and school psychology. *School Psychology Quarterly*, *28*(2), 77.

Kazdin, A. E. (1999). The meanings and measurement of clinical significance. *Journal of Consulting and Clinical Psychology*, *67*(3), 332–339. https://doi.org/10.1037/0022-006X.67.3.332

Kelly, B. (2013). Implementing implementation science: Reviewing the quest to develop methods and frameworks for effective implementation. *Journal of Neurology and Psychology*, *1*(1), 5.

Kidwai, I., & Smith, P. K. (2024). A content analysis of school anti-bullying policies in England: Signs of progress. *Educational Psychology in Practice*, *40*(1), 1–16. https://doi.org/10.1080/02667363.2023.2250258

Marley, J. (2000). Efficacy, effectiveness, efficiency. *Australian Prescriber*, *23*, 114–115.

Moir, T. (2018). Why is implementation science important for intervention design and evaluation within educational settings? *Frontiers in Education*, *3*, 61. https://doi.org/https://doi.org/10.3389/feduc.2018.00061

Pinquart, M., & Ebeling, M. (2020). Parental educational expectations and academic achievement in children and adolescents—a meta-analysis. *Educational Psychology Review*, *32*(2), 463–480.

Ranganathan, P., Pramesh, C. S., & Buyse, M. (2015). Common pitfalls in statistical analysis: Clinical versus statistical significance. *Perspectives in Clinical Research*, *6*(2229-3485 (Print)), 169–170. https://doi.org/https://doi.org/10.4103/2229-3485.159943

Section 4

Key impacts

This section in summary

Chapter 10

- Child mental health
  - o School attendance problems post-COVID-19
  - o Universal and targeted school-based mental health interventions
- Behavioural interventions for ADHD
- Anti-bullying initiatives

Chapter 11

- Inclusive education for children with SEND
- Early intervention for vulnerable preschoolers
- Teaching young readers

DOI: 10.4324/9781032691541-13

Chapter 10

Child problems in the school microsystem

Research, practice, and policy

The most significant impact of educational psychology in the UK is that practitioner educational psychologists have a statutory role to give psychological advice to local education authorities on the assessment of children and young people (CYP) with special educational needs and to contribute to their Education Health and Care Plans. These are formal legal documents that specify the support needed. In addition, educational psychologists typically contribute to systemic work in schools on a range of academic, behavioural, and mental health issues; undertake early intervention and preventive work; provide advice and carry out consultation with teachers; work collaboratively with other professionals; and support individual children who are experiencing problems, along with their families. Variations of this role are seen in countries across the world.

In this chapter and the next, we will make use of Bronfenbrenner's ecological systems theory to provide a structure to examine the impact of educational psychology on policy and practice (see Chapter 4). This chapter will focus on three areas where policy and practice is largely determined at the level of school **microsystem** concerns: child mental health, attention deficit hyperactivity disorder (ADHD), and

Microsystem Those systems that the child participates in are referred to as microsystems, for example, the family and the school.

DOI: 10.4324/9781032691541-14

reducing bullying. We'll explore school-based supports for CYP who are experiencing problems in these areas and what effective schools do to create safe, responsive environments in which CYP can thrive academically, socially, and emotionally and have their needs recognised and accommodated by school policy and classroom practice.

Child mental health

In March 2020, the World Health Organisation declared a global pandemic due to the COVID-19 virus. Schools in the UK closed as part of government lockdown measures to limit the spread of the virus. There was phased re-opening of schools in June and July for some year groups, but most children did not return to school until the start of the new term in September 2020. There was then a second lockdown in October, and although the intention was that schools remain open, some schools closed, and many parents did not send their children. During this period, schools put in place remote learning with varying degrees of effectiveness. In March 2021, mandatory school attendance was resumed but children had lost a significant amount of face-to-face learning time and opportunities for socialisation with their peers (Leahy et al., 2021). Parents were working from home, and many lost income causing financial hardship. Families were anxious about catching COVID-19 and experienced stress and disruption to their normal life routines. Being confined at home all the time affected many children's sleeping and waking patterns, reduced their opportunities for physical activity, and resulted in boredom and excessive time spent online (Raccanello et al., 2023). Families experienced bereavements due to COVID-19, and children had to learn to cope with loss and grief. The net result for school-aged CYP was impairment of opportunities for normal academic and social development and increased symptoms of anxiety and depression. Children with special educational needs, previous emotional or behavioural problems, and those living in economically disadvantaged families were especially vulnerable (Panchal et al., 2023).

How did educational psychologists help? During the pandemic lockdowns, many educational psychology services offered

> **Practitioner/professional educational psychologist** School psychologist who carries out applied work with children, school staff, carers, and families. This might be at the level of the individual child, the family, the classroom, the school, or the school district.

phone helplines. **Practitioner educational psychologists** provided telephone and online consultation to parents and professionals including teachers, special needs coordinators, speech and language therapists, and counselling to CYP. Parents, for example, could talk to a psychologist about child mental health, managing child behaviour or sibling relationships or organising a daily routine at home. When children returned to school, educational psychologists advised school staff on providing emotional support for pupil wellbeing through classroom discussions and also trained them to carry out manualised mental health interventions to build coping and resilience (Bangs et al., 2020; May et al., 2023).

Online resource 10.1 How the pandemic affected child mental health
NFER (2023). The impact of COVID-19 disruption on children and young people's wellbeing and mental health. 15 June. Available at: www.youtube.com/watch?v=OwbYNG3SY6U&t=365s (Accessed: 28 February 2025).

School attendance problems post-COVID-19

Practitioner psychologists continue to support COVID-19-related difficulties in the post-COVID-19 world. The Department for Education in England reported that 2022–2023 absence figures had doubled compared to those before the pandemic. Certainly, some families may have developed more relaxed attitudes to school absence after having their children at home for so long, but there are additional, more complex, reasons for poor attendance. Many students were absent from school due to mental health issues or due to emotionally based school avoidance concerns such as reluctance to face stressors in a school environment that they viewed as hostile, difficulties in fitting back into the school routine, or gaps in academic subjects requiring catching-up (Hamilton, 2024; McDonald et al., 2023).

Critical thinking task 10.1

What reasons for avoiding attending school can you think of? Which of these are the same/different pre-/post-pandemic?

Addressing these areas requires collective action and intervention from educators, parents, children, and practitioner educational psychologists. Before the pandemic, school psychologists already had considerable experience in carrying out evidence-based, multi-level interventions at the level of child, family, and school system to support return to school for children who experience anxiety attending school (Eklund et al., 2022; Kearney et al., 2023; Kearney & Graczyk, 2014). School staff along with the psychologist might have carried out an intervention focused on an individual child, such as individual counselling, coping and relaxation techniques, **cognitive-behavioural therapy (CBT)**, academic tutoring, drawing up a return-to-school contract, and direct work with the family. With attendance difficulties affecting more children post-pandemic, there is a need for greater emphasis on whole-school, and even district-wide, systemic approaches. Professional development activities could focus on advancing staff understanding of possible reasons for absence and what the educator's role is in supporting return to school, for example, by addressing school climate, teacher–pupil relationships, student engagement, peer relationships, and bullying (Kearney, 2021).

Cognitive-behavioural therapy (CBT) A therapeutic approach that addresses thoughts, behaviour, and feelings, assuming are all interconnected. It aims to change unhelpful thoughts as well as problematic behaviours.

Critical thinking task 10.2

Apply Bronfenbrenner's (1979) socio-ecological model in Chapter 4 to consider the micro-, meso, exo-, and macro-systems that impact on a child's life at school at different levels.

What would this model suggest for targeting interventions to help absent children return to school, post-COVID-19?

Hint: If you're stuck applying the ecological model to this issue, reading Kearney's (2021) paper can help.

Examining child mental health more widely Figures from the recent NHS survey *Mental Health of Children and Young People in England* reported 20% of CYP aged 8–16 years had a probable mental health disorder and that 445,000 people were in contact with child mental health services in November 2023, an increase from previous years. The traditional method of service delivery of mental health services in the UK is through the health service rather than through education, but this is gradually changing due to increased child mental health difficulties and lack of capacity of child and adolescent mental health services (CAMHS) to offer increased provision (Gee et al., 2020).

Universal mental health interventions

Schools then have a key preventive role to play here. One approach is to deliver school-based **universal interventions** as part of the Personal, Health and Social Education (PHSE) curriculum, with the aim of promoting positive mental health in all students. These typically make use of psychoeducational approaches that

Universal intervention This is a preventive intervention that everyone takes part in and is expected to benefit from. Individuals are not selected to take part based on any particular indicators or screening, in contrast to targeted intervention.

teach CYP ways of coping with anxiety, how to understand themselves better and develop resilience, and how to manage difficult emotions, mindfulness, and assertiveness training. Such approaches often make use of principles of **positive psychology** (see Chapter 6) or CBT (Bradshaw et al., 2021).

Positive psychology This is about enhancing subjective experiences such as well-being and happiness; optimism for the future; and personal traits like perseverance.

Who though should carry out mental health intervention in schools? This is a significant implementation issue. Teachers are likely to lack the necessary knowledge, experience, and skillset for this. Practitioner educational psychologists have been involved in short-term mental health projects in schools, but where this to become a regular element of the curriculum relying on external personnel for programme delivery has implications for intervention cost and sustainability. A possible solution is for training to be provided to education staff by educational psychologists, reducing cost and sustainability implications (Collins et al., 2014).

How effective are universal school-based interventions?

Systematic review A process in which results from several studies on the same question are synthesised. Meta-analysis may be included as part of a systematic review.

A **systematic review** of 12 studies in UK primary and secondary schools reported modest effects (Mackenzie & Williams, 2018). The small number of studies reflects the review's inclusion criterion, for example, that there needed to be pre-and post-test measures using validated instruments. Many more mental health interventions are carried out in schools whose outcomes are not subject to methodologically rigorous evaluation. Additionally, the authors suggest that for universal interventions it might be better to measure a wider range of relevant outcome measures such as school attendance, academic outcomes such as exam performance, and referral rates to CAMHS. They report that barriers to implementation (see Chapter 9) especially with respect to consistent and regular delivery of programmes as in the programme manual were often an issue.

Universal mental health screening

Another strategy to improve child mental health is that of universal mental health screening in schools. Humphrey and Wigelsworth (2016) present a convincing argument for this. This aims to identify young people at risk of mental health difficulties and then provide early **targeted intervention** before these become problematic. It is not yet a commonly used approach mainly due to current lack of practitioner educational psychologists as necessary human resource to organise and follow up screening and provide appropriate psychological support for those identified from the screening as at risk of mental health disorder. Burns and Rapee (2022) argue that effective implementation of school mental health screening programmes would need governmental backing as national policy and government resourcing.

Targeted intervention Individuals who are perceived at risk are selected for this intervention in contrast to universal intervention where everyone takes part.

Targeted mental health intervention

A possible follow-up from universal screening might be school-based mental health intervention targeted at only at students identified as at risk by the screening or those who are already experiencing mental health difficulties. What do we know about the effectiveness of targeted school-based interventions? A **meta-analytic** review of 45 trials

Meta-analysis Statistical method of systematically synthesising similar datasets from many studies on the same research question.

with 10–19-year-olds, mostly CBT-based programmes, found that while programmes showed reduction in symptoms of anxiety and depression immediately post-intervention, longer-term outcomes were not as positive. Benefits to depression symptoms were maintained at six-month follow-up, but this was not the case for improvements in anxiety. Also, the research team reported that interventions led by psychologists were more successful than those led by teaching staff (Gee et al., 2020). Psychologists training teachers for targeted interventions is a possible way forward, as for universal interventions.

Online resource 10.2 How effective are school mental health interventions?
Association for Child and Adolescent Mental Health Briony Gee (2020). Effectiveness of school-based interventions for adolescent depression and anxiety. 6 May. Available at: www.youtube.com/watch?v=Tx-uR6PFe0c (Accessed: 28 February 2025).

Box 10.1 Impact: FRIENDS – a universal school mental health intervention

The FRIENDS programme is designed to be delivered to all children in a class as part of the regular PHSE programme or equivalent. It was developed by Professor Paula Barrett in Australia and is recognised by the World Health Organisation as evidence-based best practice for the prevention of anxiety and depression in children. There are four age-appropriate versions for children aged 7–13, using CBT and positive psychology principles with the aim of improving coping, resilience, self-esteem, and reducing anxiety. The programmes can be delivered by health professionals, including educational psychologists, and teachers who are required to undertake a two-day training course. Regular booster sessions are recommended, and regular supervisory meetings by accredited FRIENDS trainers are held for practitioners to review sessions.

There are 10–12 weekly sessions, using games, videos, and activities to build skills depending on age. Prof Barrett explains here.

Online resource 10.3 Examples of activities in the Fun FRIENDS programme for preschool children
Sensory Learning 4 Life (2014). Fun FRIENDS Resilience Program. 5 May. Available at: www.youtube.com/watch?v=XbFCL5fuwG4 (Accessed: 28 February 2025).

Evaluation studies have reported positive outcomes for FRIENDS interventions, including longer-term follow-up. However, Ruttledge et al. (2016) noted that these typically utilised external specialist staff such as psychologists, school nurses, and research students, which raise issues about sustainability. Teacher-led preventive mental health interventions where teachers have received programme training would seem to be the way forward.

Learners with attention deficit hyperactivity disorder

ADHD Attention deficit hyperactivity disorder (ADHD) is a behavioural syndrome where children may have difficulty with concentration, attention, impulsivity, and staying in their seat.

Attention deficit hyperactivity disorder (**ADHD**) is a behavioural syndrome where children may have difficulty in concentrating on their classwork and keeping their attention focused. They may be hyperactive and find sitting still in class a challenge. Behaviour may be impulsive with children interrupting or calling out while the teacher is explaining the task. Symptoms can vary in severity. If the same criteria are used internationally for identification, then ADHD is thought to affect roughly 5% of the school population globally. It is more common in boys than girls, and more common in younger children than older, although this could be due to under-diagnosis in these groups. Differences in reported prevalence across countries internationally, however, are likely to be due to their different diagnostic procedures rather than to numbers of children affected. There is good evidence that medication is effective in improving symptoms although it is not successful for everyone, and the longer-term effects of these pharmacological interventions are not yet clear (Coghill et al., 2023; Coghill et al., 2022; Sayal et al., 2018).

Online resource 10.3 What is ADHD?

Amazing things project (2022). What is ADHD? 15 November. Available at: www.youtube.com/watch?v=1t9UHQgtDfU (Accessed: 28 February 2025).

ADHD in school

The classroom is a particularly challenging environment for children with ADHD as they are expected to sit in their seat, listen, and pay attention for a huge part of their day (DuPaul et al., 2014). Indeed, Pedersen et al. (2020) found that adolescents' ADHD symptoms were worse on school days compared to days when the young person was not at school and worse in the afternoon than the morning. Persistent behaviour problems have a harmful effect on the child's performance both academically and socially and are disruptive to other children in the class. Dealing with this provides a challenge to teachers and support staff (DuPaul & Jimerson, 2014). There is, however, evidence for the effectiveness of **non-pharmacological interventions** that can be applied in school (Hodgson et al., 2014). Furthermore, there is some evidence that many parents and carers prefer behavioural and psychosocial interventions to medication (Schatz et al., 2015).

Non-pharmacological interventions These are intervention approaches that do not use medications. Behaviour management and cognitive-behavioural therapy are examples as are exercise and sleep.

Non-pharmacological educational psychology interventions

Behaviour management is a non-pharmacological approach that works and is commonly used in schools. This approach uses learning theory principles of contingency management to reinforce desired behaviours and reduce unwanted behaviours such as jumping out of their seat when they should be sitting working or attending to the teacher. For example, if the child completes their maths worksheet within the maths class period, the teacher can recognise this with praise or a small reward. Charts are often used to record target behaviours that have been agreed with the young person.

A practitioner educational psychologist might similarly teach parents how to use this approach at home. Together with parents and child, they can identify desired behaviours such as sitting at the table throughout a meal and decide on a small reward to reinforce (encourage) that good behaviour. Furthermore, psychoeducational approaches with teachers, with parents, and indeed with the children themselves are an important intervention element (Moore et al., 2019). These allow their beliefs about the condition and their beliefs about the likelihood of intervention success to be explored. This is important because, beliefs, attitudes, and **attributions** can interact with the implementation of the intervention and influence the outcome (see Chapter 4).

Attribution Explanation of what caused an outcome and why it happened.

Critical thinking task 10.3

You are a special educational needs coordinator (SENCO) in a secondary school. You have responsibility for overseeing the provision of support for children with special educational needs. You have been notified that Blair, a 13-year-old boy, whose behaviour in class has always been problematic, has been given a diagnosis of ADHD by the local neurodevelopmental team whose assessment you contributed information to. Teachers report his attention span is short, he doesn't seem to listen to instructions, and he tends to get distracted and not complete tasks he has been set.

How might you advise subject teachers to make adjustments for Blair?

The Division of Educational and Child Psychology of The British Psychological Society produced a briefing paper in 2022 that provides detailed guidance on evidence-informed interventions for CYP with difficulties with attention, hyperactivity, and impulsivity that can be implemented by practitioner educational psychologists and schools. Recommended assessment includes gathering information from the young person, education staff, and parents to build an all-round picture of the nature and extent of relationship and learning difficulties at school and at home. The practitioner educational psychologist might also carry out structured observation in class to get an idea of the contexts in which difficulties tend to occur. This holistic assessment feeds into an agreed intervention plan which education staff will manage in school.

In addition to using positive reinforcement as described above, educational psychology recommendations can include modifying the environment to consider where is best for the child to sit in class, for example, close to teacher, away from distraction of windows. There may be specific tools that can help individuals such as use of timers to help focus attention on timeframes for task completion, breathing exercises for self-calming, and fidget tools to keep hands busy. Teachers can actively engage the child by giving them tasks to do, providing visual schedules so that child knows what's next and where they are supposed to be, and breaking tasks into small steps. They can set clear rules and expectations in their classes and build warm, positive relationships in their classes, where learners feel safe and understood. Strategies for students with ADHD can be embedded within a whole-school policy for developing an ethos and culture that benefits all students and not only those with ADHD.

UK policy formally recognises ADHD as a disability, and so children with ADHD will be added to the school's Special Educational Needs and Disabilities (SEND) register. The school is then required to make reasonable adjustments to ensure that the child with SEND is not at a disadvantage, compared to other children. There will be consultation among teachers, parents, and the educational psychologist to identify the child's needs and barriers to learning. Further assessment may be carried out, and an intervention plan will be agreed to support the child academically and socially, with regular monitoring and review. There is more about the broader area of inclusion of children with SEND in Chapter 11.

How schools tackle bullying

Policy in principle

In Chapter 5, we covered several theories of **bullying** to

Bullying Repeated threatening or aggressive behaviour towards one or more individuals in which there is an imbalance of power. Can be direct or indirect.

demonstrate educational psychology's understanding of the phenomenon. In this chapter, we now examine the impact of these understandings for policy and practice. UNESCO's (2022) strategy for health and wellbeing in schools makes it clear that schools throughout the world are required to ensure a safe learning environment, free from violence and bullying. Schools are expected to have measures in place to address this and furthermore to strengthen these. Anti-bullying policies are often part of wider behaviour strategy. Their purpose is to provide a framework for the school's actions. For example, advice to English schools from the Department for Education (DfE) in 2017 clarifies for educators that there is a range of behaviours considered to be bullying, beyond the physical. It explains that bullying is repeated hurtful behaviour, that is intentional, and that it can be emotional or even take place outside the school day and the school premises as in **cyberbullying**. Schools then need to be able to recognise this wide range of behaviours and be prepared to tackle them through their policies.

Cyberbullying Carrying out verbally threatening or harassing behaviour using digital means, such as text messages, email, social media sites. May be viewed as a form of indirect bullying.

Policy in practice

How well do school policies provide an anti-bullying framework for action? Kidwai and Smith (2024) surveyed 200 English schools and found that most mentioned the range of different kinds of bullying, the need for a safe school environment, and that incidents would be recorded. However, few flagged up the important role of non-teaching staff when they were aware of bullying, few mentioned how to help those bullying change their behaviour, and few school policies specified what powers the school has to act in instances of cyberbullying and out-of-school bullying. This means that there are numerous schools lacking an intervention plan to deal with these behaviours. Of course, identifying issues in the school policy is only a first step to addressing bullying and does not mean that this in itself is necessarily followed by a decrease in bullying behaviour in the school (Purdy & Smith, 2016).

Anti-bullying intervention

Achieving positive change depends on competent implementation of the policy and putting in place evidence-informed interventions. Schools that are most successful in reducing bullying not only have policies in place to respond to bullying at an individual level when it happens, but importantly, they focus on whole-school approaches to the prevention of bullying, they implement anti-bullying rules at classroom level, their teachers are trained in methods of bullying prevention and classroom management, and the school delivers an anti-bullying programme with a structured curriculum and opportunities for activities and discussion (Gaffney et al., 2021a). Gaffney et al. (2021b) carried out a systematic review of 100 programmes and concluded that school-based anti-bullying intervention programmes are successful in reducing bullying by around 15–20%. While this is a statistically small effect size, if we think of it in terms of the numbers of children not experiencing bullying because of the intervention, it becomes significant in practice. We'll consider here three examples of programmes, one from Norway, one from Finland, and one from Italy. Gaffney et al. (2021a,b) describe many more.

The Olweus Bullying Prevention Programme (OBPP)

Dan Olweus can be considered the 'father' of the systematic study of bullying (see Chapter 5). Olweus and colleagues developed the OBPP in Norway in the late 1980s, following the suicide of three Norwegian boys. It is a prototype for other later anti-bullying programmes. It aims to restructure the school environment to reduce existing bullying problems, prevent new bullying, and improve peer relationships. It is a whole-school **universal** programme which means that all pupils participate, and alongside this are additional targeted individual interventions for bullies and victims. It is a multi-level intervention at the level of the school, the classroom, the individual, and the wider community. At the school level, the OBPP advocates the importance of creating a warm, nurturing school environment that recognises the danger of violence and bullying and reduces opportunities and rewards for bullying behaviours. There is a school coordination committee which is responsible for overseeing the OBPP. There are also class level components with clear rules about bullying specified and enforced and weekly class meetings. Common barriers to implementing the programme are that school staff and parents do not view bullying as a concern, overestimate how effectively victims can stop bullying without adult involvement, and time constraints on staff participations in the two-day training programme (Olweus & Limber, 2010). The OBPP is the oldest anti-bullying programme, and there is a substantial body of international evidence of its success in reducing bullying. It is more effective the longer it is place (Limber et al., 2018; Olweus et al., 2019; Ossa et al., 2021).

KiVa

KiVa is a Finnish programme developed by Christina Salmivalli at University of Turku. Like OBPP, it also takes a multi-level approach. It is based on **participant role theory** (see Chapter 5) and focuses on changing the bystander's behaviour and the bully's behaviour. The focus is on changing the culture of the school and increasing awareness and empathy in students by universal actions that are delivered as class lessons. There are also what KiVa refers to as 'indicated' actions which are specifically for the bully and the victim

> **Participant role theory** Recognition that in addition to bully and victim there are other roles in bullying: reinforcer (laughs or encourages), assistant (joins in), defender of victim (helps victim), and bystander (aware of bullying but ignores it).

The KiVa programme comprises ten structured lessons with discussions, role play, video, and group activities where they learn about being part of a team, learn about how groups work, learn about how to deal with emotions, bullying, and the role of the bystander, and what they can do to reduce bullying (Hutchings & Clarkson, 2015). A school carrying out the programme promotes itself as a KiVa school with posters and information on its website and staff wearing KiVa-branded waistcoats at break.

Online resource 10.4 The KiVa programme
World Anti-Bullying Forum (2022). KiVa anti-bullying programme 8 July. Available at: www.youtube.com/watch?v=jXQws5WTdKk&t=89s (Accessed: 28 February 2025).

KiVa is widely used in schools across Finland and has demonstrated good outcomes in Finland, in Italy, and in the Netherlands (Huitsing et al., 2020; Kärnä et al., 2011; Nocentini & Menesini, 2016). It was reported as less successful in a trial in Wales where there were problems with **implementation fidelity** (Axford et al., 2020). Moreover, there may be cultural differences between countries that mean that what works in one country will not necessarily work similarly in another. For this reason, it is currently being evaluated for use in the UK setting (Clarkson et al., 2022).

Implementation fidelity The extent to which an intervention is implemented as intended and how faithful the actual programme delivery is to its original plan.

Summary

This chapter focused on policy and practice on three specific challenges for schools: mental health, bullying, and ADHD. It showed the impact of educational psychology on a range of school-level preventive and supportive strategies and initiatives that aim to promote positive mental health, that aim to foster an anti-bullying school culture, and that support students with ADHD.

References/Further reading

Axford, N., Bjornstad, G., Clarkson, S., Ukoumunne, O. C., Wrigley, Z., Matthews, J. ... Hutchings, J. (2020). The effectiveness of the KiVa bullying prevention program in Wales, UK: Results from a pragmatic cluster randomized controlled trial. *Prevention Science*, *21*(5), 615–626.

Bangs, R., Ní, B. E., Christie, B., & Eoin, K. (2020). Response to Covid-19: How do schools support children following a crisis? *Educational Psychology in Scotland*, *20*(20), 6–12. https://doi.org/10.53841/bpsepis.2020.20.1.6

Bradshaw, M., Gericke, H., Coetzee, B. J., Stallard, P., Human, S., & Loades, M. (2021). Universal school-based mental health programmes in low- and middle-income countries: A systematic review and narrative synthesis. *Preventive Medicine*, *143*, 106317. https://doi.org/10.1016/j.ypmed.2020.106317

Bronfenbrenner, U. (1979). *The ecology of human development: Experiments by nature and design*. Harvard University Press.

Burns, J. R., & Rapee, R. M. (2022). Barriers to universal mental health screening in schools: The perspective of school psychologists. *Journal of Applied School Psychology*, *38*(3), 223–240. https://doi.org/10.1080/15377903.2021.1941470

Clarkson, S., Bowes, L., Coulman, E., Broome, M. R., Cannings-John, R., Charles, J. M. ... the Stand Together, T. (2022). The UK stand together trial: Protocol for a multicentre cluster randomised controlled trial to evaluate the effectiveness and cost-effectiveness of KiVa to reduce bullying in primary schools. *BMC Public Health*, *22*(1), 608. https://doi.org/10.1186/s12889-022-12642-x

Coghill, D., Banaschewski, T., Cortese, S., Asherson, P., Brandeis, D., Buitelaar, J. ... Simonoff, E. (2023). The management of ADHD in children and adolescents: Bringing evidence to the clinic: Perspective from the European ADHD Guidelines Group (EAGG). *European Child & Adolescent Psychiatry*, *32*(8), 1337–1361. https://doi.org/10.1007/s00787-021-01871-x

Coghill, D., Du, Y., Jiang, W., Xian, Lu, D., Qian, Y. ... Su, L. (2022). A novel school-based approach to screening for attention deficit hyperactivity disorder. *European Child & Adolescent Psychiatry*, *31*(6), 909–917. https://doi.org/10.1007/s00787-021-01721-w

Collins, S., Woolfson, L. M., & Durkin, K. (2014). Effects on coping skills and anxiety of a universal school-based mental health intervention delivered in Scottish primary schools. *School Psychology International*, *35*(1), 85–100. https://doi.org/10.1177/0143034312469157

DuPaul, G. J., & Jimerson, S. R. (2014). Assessing, understanding, and supporting students with ADHD at school: Contemporary science, practice, and policy. *School Psychology Quarterly*, *29*(4), 379–384. https://doi.org/10.1037/spq0000104

DuPaul, G. J., Reid, R., Anastopoulos, A. D., & Power, T. J. (2014). Assessing ADHD symptomatic behaviors and functional impairment in school settings: Impact of student and teacher characteristics. *School Psychology Quarterly*, *29*(4), 409–421. https://doi.org/10.1037/spq0000095

Eklund, K., Burns, M. K., Oyen, K., DeMarchena, S., & McCollom, E. M. (2022). Addressing chronic absenteeism in schools: A meta-analysis of evidence-based interventions. *School Psychology Review*, *51*(1), 95–111. https://doi.org/10.1080/2372966X.2020.1789436

Gaffney, H., Ttofi, M. M., & Farrington, D. P. (2021a). What works in anti-bullying programs? Analysis of effective intervention components. *Journal of School Psychology*, *85*, 37–56.

Gaffney, H., Ttofi, M. M., & Farrington, D. P. (2021b). Effectiveness of school-based programs to reduce bullying perpetration and victimization: An updated systematic review and meta-analysis. *Campbell Systematic Reviews*, *17*(2), e1143. https://doi.org/10.1002/cl2.1143

Gee, B., Reynolds, S., Carroll, B., Orchard, F., Clarke, T., Martin, D. … Pass, L. (2020). Practitioner Review: Effectiveness of indicated school-based interventions for adolescent depression and anxiety – a meta-analytic review. *Journal of Child Psychology and Psychiatry*, *61*(7), 739–756. https://doi.org/10.1111/jcpp.13209

Hamilton, L. G. (2024). Emotionally based school avoidance in the aftermath of the COVID-19 pandemic: Neurodiversity, agency and belonging in school. *Education Sciences*, *14*(2), 156.

Hodgson, K., Hutchinson, A. D., & Denson, L. (2014). Nonpharmacological treatments for ADHD: A meta-analytic review. *Journal of Attention Disorders*, *18*(4), 275–282. https://doi.org/10.1177/1087054712444732

Huitsing, G., Lodder, G. M., Browne, W. J., Oldenburg, B., Van der Ploeg, R., & Veenstra, R. (2020). A large-scale replication of the effectiveness of the KiVa antibullying program: A randomized controlled trial in the Netherlands. *Prevention Science*, *21*, 627–638.

Humphrey, N., & Wigelsworth, M. (2016). Making the case for universal school-based mental health screening. *Emotional and Behavioural Difficulties*, *21*(1), 22–42. https://doi.org/10.1080/13632752.2015.1120051

Hutchings, J., & Clarkson, S. (2015). Introducing and piloting the KiVa bullying prevention programme in the UK. *Educational and Child Psychology*, *32*(1), 49–61.

Kearney, C. A. (2021). Integrating systemic and analytic approaches to school attendance problems: Synergistic frameworks for research and policy directions. *Child & Youth Care Forum*, *50*(4), 701–742. https://doi.org/10.1007/s10566-020-09591-0

Kearney, C. A., Dupont, R., Fensken, M., & Gonzálvez, C. (2023). School attendance problems and absenteeism as early warning signals: Review and implications for health-based protocols and school-based practices. *Frontiers in Education*, *8*, 1–1253595.

Kearney, C. A., & Graczyk, P. (2014). A response to intervention model to promote school attendance and decrease school absenteeism. *Child*

& Youth Care Forum, *43*(1), 1–25. https://doi.org/10.1007/s10566-013-9222-1

Kidwai, I., & Smith, P. K. (2024). A content analysis of school anti-bullying policies in England: Signs of progress. *Educational Psychology in Practice*, *40*(1), 1–16. https://doi.org/10.1080/02667363.2023.2250258

Kärnä, A., Voeten, M., Little, T. D., Poskiparta, E., Kaljonen, A., & Salmivalli, C. (2011). A large-scale evaluation of the KiVa antibullying program: Grades 4–6. *Child Development*, *82*(1), 311–330.

Leahy, F., Newton, P., & Khan, A. (2021). *Learning during the pandemic: Quantifying lost time*. Ofqual.

Limber, S. P., Olweus, D., Wang, W., Masiello, M., & Breivik, K. (2018). Evaluation of the Olweus Bullying Prevention Program: A large scale study of U.S. students in grades 3–11. *Journal of School Psychology*, *69*, 56–72. https://doi.org/10.1016/j.jsp.2018.04.004

Mackenzie, K., & Williams, C. (2018). Universal, school-based interventions to promote mental and emotional well-being: What is being done in the UK and does it work? A systematic review. *BMJ open*, *8*(9), e022560.

May, F., Schaffer, G. E., Allen, K., Berger, E., von Hagen, A., Hill, V. ... Reupert, A. (2023). Perspectives of practising school psychologists during COVID-19: A multi-country, mixed methods investigation. *School Psychology International*, *44*(0143-0343 (Print)), 447–467. https://doi.org/10.1177/01430343221137716

McDonald, B., Lester, K. J., & Michelson, D. (2023). 'She didn't know how to go back': School attendance problems in the context of the COVID-19 pandemic—A multiple stakeholder qualitative study with parents and professionals. *British Journal of Educational Psychology*, *93*(1), 386–401. https://doi.org/10.1111/bjep.12562

Moore, D. A., Richardson, M., Gwernan-Jones, R., Thompson-Coon, J., Stein, K., Rogers, M. ... Ford, T. J. (2019). Non-pharmacological interventions for ADHD in school settings: An overarching synthesis of systematic reviews. *Journal of Attention Disorders*, *23*(3), 220–233. https://doi.org/10.1177/1087054715573994

Nocentini, A., & Menesini, E. (2016). KiVa anti-bullying program in Italy: Evidence of effectiveness in a randomized control trial. *Prevention Science*, *17*, 1012–1023.

Olweus, D., & Limber, S. P. (2010). Bullying in school: Evaluation and dissemination of the Olweus Bullying Prevention Program. *American Journal of Orthopsychiatry*, *80*(1), 124.

Olweus, D., Limber, S. P., & Breivik, K. (2019). Addressing specific forms of bullying: A large-scale evaluation of the Olweus bullying prevention program. *International Journal of Bullying Prevention*, *1*, 70–84.

Ossa, F. C., Jantzer, V., Eppelmann, L., Parzer, P., Resch, F., & Kaess, M. (2021). Effects and moderators of the Olweus bullying prevention program (OBPP) in Germany. *European Child & Adolescent Psychiatry*, *30*, 1745–1754.

Panchal, U., Salazar de Pablo, G., Franco, M., Moreno, C., Parellada, M., Arango, C., & Fusar-Poli, P. (2023). The impact of COVID-19 lockdown on child and adolescent mental health: Systematic review. *European Child & Adolescent Psychiatry*, 32(7), 1151–1177.

Pedersen, S. L., Kennedy, T. M., Joseph, H. M., Riston, S. J., Kipp, H. L., & Molina, B. S. G. (2020). Real-world changes in adolescents' ADHD symptoms within the day and across school and non-school days. *Journal of Abnormal Child Psychology*, *48*(12), 1543–1553. https://doi.org/10.1007/s10802-020-00695-8

Purdy, N., & Smith, P. K. (2016). A content analysis of school anti-bullying policies in Northern Ireland. *Educational Psychology in Practice*, *32*(3), 281–295. https://doi.org/10.1080/02667363.2016.1161599

Raccanello, D., Rocca, E., Vicentini, G., & Brondino, M. (2023). Eighteen months of COVID-19 pandemic through the lenses of self or others: A meta-analysis on children and adolescents' mental health. *Child & Youth Care Forum*, *52*(4), 737–760. https://doi.org/10.1007/s10566-022-09706-9

Ruttledge, R., Devitt, E., Greene, G., Mullany, M., Charles, E., Frehill, J., & Moriarty, M. (2016). A randomised controlled trial of the FRIENDS for life emotional resilience programme delivered by teachers in Irish primary schools. *Educational & Child Psychology*, *33*(2), 69–89.

Sayal, K., Prasad, V., Daley, D., Ford, T., & Coghill, D. (2018). ADHD in children and young people: Prevalence, care pathways, and service provision. *The Lancet Psychiatry*, *5*, 175–186. https://doi.org/10.1016/S2215-0366(17)30167-0

Schatz, N. K., Fabiano, G. A., Cunningham, C. E., dosReis, S., Waschbusch, D. A., Jerome, S. ... Morris, K. L. (2015). Systematic review of patients' and parents' preferences for ADHD treatment options and processes of care. *The Patient-Patient-Centered Outcomes Research*, *8*, 483–497.

Chapter 11

Initiatives from exosystems

Research, practice, and policy

In this chapter as in the previous one, we will make use of Bronfenbrenner's ecological systems theory (see Chapter 4) to provide a structure to examine the impact of educational psychology on policy and practice.

> **Microsystem** The systems that the child participates in directly are referred to as microsystems, for example, the family and the school.

> **Exosystem** This is a system such as the district council that the child has no direct contact with but whose policies affect the child's experience in school.

In Chapter 10, we looked at topics within the school **microsystem,** but here we move beyond the school to consider three big issues where policy and practice is determined at the level of the **exosystem**, by government or local authority systems that are external to the school. We will examine the role of educational psychology in research, policy and practice regarding inclusive education for children with special educational needs and disabilities (SEND), teaching young readers, and early intervention for vulnerable preschoolers.

Inclusive education for learners with special educational needs and disabilities

The aim of inclusive education today is for schools to change their systems and practices to accommodate diversity of ability, gender,

DOI: 10.4324/9781032691541-15

ethnicity, family structure, and lifestyle. Influences on the inclusive education paradigm from a social justice perspective included the civil rights movement in the USA, the disability rights movement, and recognition that children with special needs had an equal right to access education in their local school just as their neighbours did. Educational influences included UK research exploring what makes an effective school. Implications of this work for children with **SEND** were that if we could work out how to improve schools, this would make them more effective for a wider range of learners. A further educational influence on inclusive education was a nagging concern about whether children's special educational needs were really better catered for in segregated special schools as was claimed (Marks Woolfson, 2024). We will return to this last point shortly.

SEND Commonly used acronym for special educational needs and disabilities.

Box 11.1 Impact: educational psychologists and the development of inclusive education

As discussed in the previous chapter, a significant impact of educational psychology is the statutory role of **practitioner educational psychologists** in the assessment of children and young people with SEND. A major element of this role is in promoting and supporting national inclusive education policies

Practitioner/professional educational psychologist School psychologist carries out applied work with children, school staff, carers, and families. This might be at the level of the individual child, the family, the classroom, the school, or the school district.

for children with SEND as these evolved through the years (BPS DECP, 2022).

Until the 1970s, children with severe learning difficulties were viewed as 'ineducable' and only then were they brought into the education system but educated separately. Children who were categorised by educational psychologists as 'handicapped' (in the language of that time) were required to attend segregated special schools which were thought to better cater to their specific needs. However, in 1978, a committee chaired by Baroness Warnock questioned this over-simplistic classification and introduced the concept of special educational needs.

Professional educational psychologists had a key role in the statutory assessment of educational need and how the local authority might meet this need. For some children, this could mean 'integration' into a mainstream school if the school felt able to accommodate those needs. For others, the need would be met, as before, by segregated special schooling. Since the 1980s, though, this concept has developed from the limited aspiration of integration of the few to the much wider one of schools recognising the diversity of the student population and aiming to provide an inclusive education system that accommodates all learners.

Educational psychologists' role

Practitioner educational psychologists have been involved throughout the historical implementation of government integration and inclusion policies, by assessing special educational needs and supporting learners, teachers, and parents. In present day policy, the SEND system in the UK requires educational psychologists to contribute to Education, Health and Care (EHC) plans. The EHC plan is a legal policy document for children who have additional needs that cannot be met by the school. It specifies the learner's needs and the support required to meet them to achieve their goals. US school psychologists have a similar role in writing Individualised Education Programmes. In both countries, there are significant backlogs for children with SEND who need additional support because of lack of educational/school psychologists to carry out the statutory assessments (DfE, 2023; Sohn, 2024). Without sufficient educational psychologists and sufficient financial resourcing, the current SEND system breaks down. Recent reports recommend the system cannot cope with the demands on it and needs radical reform (Isos Partnership, 2024; UK Parliament Public Accounts Committee, 2025). In January 2025, two expert panels that include psychologists, educators, and administrators were appointed to advise the government on how to mend the broken SEND system and make schools more inclusive.

Theory in the inclusive classroom – child

Educational psychology theories have had a significant impact on practice in this field. For example, when educators break down learning tasks for children with SEND into small achievable steps with rewards to reinforce good work, they are applying principles of **behaviourism**. **Constructivist theory** points teachers to arranging structured learning experiences to help learners with SEND construct their own understandings. Vygotsky's **social constructivist theory** as discussed in Chapter 4 guides the educator's social interactional role where effective teachers interact with learners in inclusive classrooms, asking pertinent questions,

Behaviourism Theory of learning that views behaviours as being learned through reinforcement by environmental stimuli.

Constructivism Children actively try to make meaning from their experiences to build their own understanding of the world.

Social constructivism While the constructivist approach to the child's development views the child as constructing their own understanding of the world through active interaction with the environment, social constructivism regards learning to be the result of learner interactions with the social and cultural context of their environment.

providing prompts and modelling next steps thus supporting the child to new understandings by leading them through Vygotsky's **zone of proximal development.** Similarly, Bruner's **scaffolding** guides new learning.

Zone of proximal development The difference between what children can achieve unaided and what they can do with assistance from someone more expert.

Scaffolding A teaching style in which an adult structures the learning task and directs the learner to critical features, so encouraging the learner towards greater success than would have been achieved alone.

Theory in the inclusive classroom – teacher

While the child is central to educational psychology and is the focus of inclusive education, educational psychology research is also very interested in the teacher and how to improve the teacher element of the teacher-student learning interaction. Ajzen's (1991) **theory of planned behaviour (TPB)** (Ajzen, 1991) which is typically used to examine beliefs about health behaviours such as smoking, exercise, or diet has also been applied in educational psychology studies to examine teachers' beliefs about inclusion of learners with SEND and their inclusive teaching behaviours. TPB applied to inclusive teaching examines teachers' *attitudes* to inclusion, *subjective norm* (teacher beliefs about how their colleagues view inclusive teaching behaviours), and *perceived behavioural control* (how easy or

Theory of planned behaviour This theory asserts that behaviour can be predicted by beliefs about how others view the behaviour (subjective norms), how easy or difficult it is to carry out the behaviour (perceived behavioural control), and the individual's intention to perform the behaviour.

difficult it is for them to carry out inclusive teaching practices). The theory then explores how these factors influence teachers' *intention* to perform inclusive teaching and their influences on inclusive teacher *behaviour.*

Research studies usually use a statistical technique called multiple regression to identify which of these best predicts inclusive teaching behaviour. This line of research indicates that subjective norm factors such as the ethos of the school, social pressure from colleagues, and expectations communicated by the head teacher are important in promoting inclusive behaviours in the classroom. Going even further back in the life of a teacher, before they even arrive at their first professional position, greater practical pre-service training on working with learners with SEND is needed to help develop positive attitudes and feelings of self-efficacy (perceived behavioural control) towards inclusive teaching in their classrooms (MacFarlane & Marks Woolfson, 2013; Urton et al., 2023; Wilson et al., 2016; Yan & Sin, 2014). This work indicates there are distal factors that are beyond teaching plans and immediate teacher classroom practices, that influence teacher behaviour regarding inclusion of children with SEND, and that can themselves be the target of professional development to change what then ultimately happens in the classroom.

Critical thinking task 11.1

Look over Key Theories in Part 2 and identify three other theories that are used in inclusive classrooms and consider how they are applied.

Is inclusive education effective?

While all learners have the right to be educated in their local mainstream school, research has explored a key question here: Do children with SEND do better academically in mainstream schools than in special schools? Methodologically this is a tricky question to answer.

> **Inclusive education** Where mainstream schools develop systems and practices that accommodate diversity of ability, gender, ethnicity, family structure, and lifestyle.

Critical thinking task 11.2

Design a study to evaluate whether learners with SEND do better academically in inclusive mainstream schools?
Think carefully about:

- *Selection of participants for the mainstream intervention group*
- *Selection of participants for comparison group*

What are the difficulties in designing such a study?
Hint: If you're stuck, Chapter 9 of Educational psychology: The impact of psychological research on education can help (Marks Woolfson, 2011).

Findings suggest that within SEND systems as they are currently, there are either some small positive academic effects of inclusive education for children with SEND or no difference between special and mainstream settings (Dell'Anna et al., 2022; Ruijs & Peetsma, 2009). A related question is about social outcomes. Parents often want their child with SEND to attend the local mainstream school as they anticipate developmental benefits and increased opportunities for social interactions and friendships with other neighbourhood children. Research findings suggest that while there might be improved social development for children with SEND in mainstream, disappointingly there is less evidence of greater social participation with peers (Dell'Anna et al., 2022).

Teaching beginning readers

Learning to read is one of the most important, transformative tasks for children. Reading opens doors to accessing the wider school curriculum, advances children's progress through the education system, and promotes independence for children to follow their own interests outside school. How best to teach early readers has therefore been a major focus for educators, educational psychology research, and governmental policies. The topic has always been controversial with support for different methods of teaching reading. This controversy is emotively known as 'the reading wars'.

To discuss teaching beginning readers, we need first to familiarise ourselves with some reading vocabulary.

Online resource 11.1 Clarifying terms: phoneme, grapheme, and phonics
The FIVE from FIVE reading project (2019). Phonemes and graphemes. 17 October. Available at: www.youtube.com/watch?v=eMgGOH4BqFs (Accessed: 28 February 2025).

There are three main approaches to the teaching of reading (Solity & Vousden, 2009; Wyse & Bradbury, 2022):

1 *Phonics first* Here, the emphasis is on children learning the relationship between sounds and printed letters before they read authentic texts. There is a significant body of educational psychology evidence that the systematic teaching of **phonics,** to make the link between spoken sounds and printed alphabetic letters, is necessary for beginning readers (Ehri, 2020; Ehri, Nunes, Stahl, et al., 2001; Goswami & Bryant, 2016; Hatcher et al., 2004). **Phonemes** are the smallest units of sound; e.g., the word 'dog' is made up of three phonemes, /d/ /o/ /g/. The ability to discriminate and manipulate phonemes is an important foundational skill for later acquisition of word reading and comprehension (Bond & Dykstra, 1967; Ehri, Nunes, Willows, et al., 2001).

> **Phoneme** The smallest unit of sound in a word; e.g., the word 'dog' is made up of three phonemes, /d/ /o/ /g/.

   a **Synthetic phonics** is a teaching method where beginning readers learn in a systematic sequence which sounds match with which

> **Phonics** A method of teaching beginners reading by focusing on the relationship between sounds and printed letters.

written alphabetic letters and then learn to blend (synthesise) these sounds to build them into words. Children may work on blending phonemes before they are given books. This method is often described as 'part-to-whole'.

b **Analytic phonics** also teaches the correspondence between sounds and letter (phoneme and grapheme) but does not begin with sounding out and blending sounds. Instead, this method begins with whole-word recognition using a graded reading book. It encourages readers to build a whole-word reading vocabulary using **look and say** and from this to recognise word patterns. Children learn about sounds by analysing similarities in the beginnings and endings of whole-words. It can be considered as 'whole-to-part'.

Synthetic phonics An approach where beginning readers learn which sounds match with which written letters and then blend (synthesise) the sounds to build them into words.

Analytic phonics Children learn to read whole words and from these deduce sounds by recognising the sound pattern in words beginning and ending with the same sound.

Look and say This is a whole-word method of teaching reading. Children look at the whole word and learn its visual shape. By memorising the whole shape of the word, and without breaking it down into its component sounds, they can say (read) the word.

2 *Whole language* (also known as *real books*) Reading is ultimately about comprehension, about engaging with and understanding the meaning of written text in a pleasurable way. This principle is central to the whole-language method, rather than comprehension being an activity that learners progress to after mastering phonics. So instead of teaching reading through

out-of-context phonics and then by means of a graded difficulty reading scheme, children are expected to learn to read naturally. This approach uses children's literature through meaningful engagement with language and reading books that interest them, and in this way increase motivation and helps them learn about sounds through examples in the books. This method of teaching reading has often been blamed for a drop in standards, but it should be noted that teachers who use this approach now tend to also incorporate phonics teaching within it (Torgerson et al., 2019; Wyse & Bradbury, 2022).

3 *Balanced instruction* This advocates a balance between systematic teaching of phonic decoding strategies and reading real books to build comprehension skills and a wider engagement with literacy. Balanced instruction contextualises the systematic teaching of phonic skills by embedding them into the reading of children's books, both specially designed decodable 'reading' books for reading practice with adult help and 'real' books (children's literature and poems). This method involves discussion of the meaning of a story, general language enrichment activities, and integration of skills learned into children's writing and spelling (Freppon & Dahl, 1998). Effective teachers know that one method is not suitable for all learners and that a variety of approaches is needed (Glazzard & Stones, 2020). The wide range of different learning activities contained in balanced instruction gives teachers the flexibility to use their expertise to take account of individual learner difficulties and select appropriate reading tasks, rather than instructing the child struggling with phonics only with more intensive phonics within a one-size-fits-all programme.

Online resource 11.2 Reading wars

Storied (2024). You were probably taught to read wrong. 19 September. Available at: www.youtube.com/watch?v=bGsNcFfezLM (Accessed: 28 February 2025).

Policy recommendations

In 2006, a governmental review in England chaired by Sir Jim Rose recommended that schools place emphasis on synthetic phonics as their central method for teaching phonics and teaching reading. Since then, this approach has been mandated in subsequent national strategies, currently in DfE's *Reading Framework*. Compliance and progress with the strategy are followed up with phonic screening tests in the early primary school years. Wyse and Bradbury (2022) analysed the national curriculum policies of a number of English-speaking countries that ranked highly in international assessments of performance of reading literacy. They categorised policies in countries, such as Canada, New Zealand, and Ireland, which performed well in these evaluations, as using the whole-language method, and Australia and USA as indicating balanced instruction. They pointed out that England was an outlier with its emphasis on synthetic phonics.

The Rose review recommendations relied heavily on studies carried out in Clackmannanshire, a small Scottish local authority (Johnston & Watson, 2004, 2005). This research appeared to demonstrate that teaching synthetic phonics was the most effective method, but there have been criticisms of the design of the research studies that cast doubt on this conclusion (Wyse & Goswami, 2008). Synthetic phonics teaching may indeed be particularly effective in countries where the language shows **orthographic consistency** (consistent phoneme–grapheme correspondence) (Landerl, 2000), that is to say, where written letters always have the same sounds. This is not the case with English; for example, compare the different ways we read the letters '*ough*' in th*ough*t, c*ough*, th*ough*, and b*ough*. The grapheme '*ough*' is not consistent, and the reader has to learn that these printed letters represent different phonemes. Research evidence rather indicates that both analytic and synthetic phonics can produce good outcomes and that it is systematic teaching of phonics that is important (Glazzard, 2017; Hatcher et al., 2004).

Orthographic consistency Written letters always have the same sounds. This is not the case in English where written letters can sound differently, e.g. pl*ea*se, br*ea*d, and gr*ea*t.

Online resource 11.3 Profs Wyse and Bradbury explaining their 2022 paper

Helen Hamlyn Centre for Pedagogy (2021). Reading wars or reading reconciliation. Prof Dominic Wyse and Prof Alice Bradbury 25 November. Available at: www.youtube.com/watch?v=bJImJ79JKNI (Accessed: 28 February 2025).

Critical thinking task 11.3

Use your library databases to read Johnston and Watson's reports on the Clackmannanshire studies comparing different methods of teaching phonics. Then read Wyse and Goswami's (2008) critique and locate other journal papers that discuss what we can conclude from the Clackmannanshire studies.

Do you agree that there is compelling evidence for synthetic phonics?

Reading wars continue. As educational psychology researchers are not in agreement, it is a significant challenge for policy makers and educators in the classroom to decide which method is best for teaching beginner readers. There is, however, currently a consensus on the importance of systematic phonics for beginning readers. It is worth noting though that there are more research studies of phonics than of other methods of teaching reading. Programmes such as balanced instruction that are more individualised and loosely formulated are difficult to evaluate for comparison purposes. There is also broad recognition among researchers that there are other skills involved in reading for meaning that need to be taught and that systematic phonics teaching can be embedded within a rich language curriculum alongside reading children's literature, developing vocabulary and comprehension skills, rather than preceding these (Brooks, 2023; Reinking et al., 2023; Wyse & Bradbury, 2022). Not all national policies take account of this yet.

Early intervention

Need for intervention

In earlier chapters, we examined research on young children's cognitive, social, and emotional development. But what about those children whose development is showing delays and who are not demonstrating school readiness skills? There has been a huge body of research on the effects on development for vulnerable children who lack the necessary educational and social opportunities for stimulation and behaviour regulation in their preschool home environment. Early development in the preschool years has been shown to influence not only school factors such as academic outcomes, behaviour and dropout, but also later life factors such as mental health, criminality, and participation in society (Marks Woolfson et al., 2013; Muennig et al., 2009; Shonkoff, 2010). Risk factors include family size; stressful life events, mother's mental health, educational attainment, and developmental beliefs; social support, unsafe neighbourhoods, and occupation of head of household. It is not any particular risk factor that predicts poor outcomes but their cumulative effects (Appleyard et al., 2005). Resilience mitigates against risk factors to promote good outcomes in spite of adversity (Luthar et al., 2000; Sameroff, 2010).

Inequalities are already evident when children start school, with disadvantaged children behind in the foundational cognitive and behavioural skills required for learning. 69% children in England did not meet the literacy levels of the recent annual national early years assessment. This has implications for poor academic attainment in later school years and a longer-term trajectory of underachievement and underemployment (Davies et al., 2016; Ryan et al., 2013).

Family influences

We see how important family influences in the home environment are for young children's development and for building resilience. These are influences such as the quality and warmth of parent–child interaction, the extent to which parenting provides stimulating intellectual and social, age-appropriate experiences for the child, and the extent to which the parent ensures the child is healthy and safe (Guralnick, 2006; Sameroff, 2010). Literacy experiences arranged by parents both within and outside the home have an impact on readiness for reading when children start school and also later life outcomes. A survey carried out by the National Literacy Trust shows that parents are reading less with their children, talking, playing, and singing less with them now than in 2019 and that this societal drop in family engagement in opportunities for language development is likely to affect socio-economically disadvantaged children even more strongly (Picton et al., 2024).

Interventions

The main psychological theories that have influenced early intervention programmes are **social learning** (Bandura & Walters, 1977), **social ecological model** (Bronfenbrenner, 1979) (see Chapter 4), **transactional model** (Sameroff, 2009), and concepts of vulnerability and resilience (Rutter, 2013) (Shonkoff, 2010). These theories all emphasise that the child's development depends on a complex set of dynamic factors between the child and its social context. Governmental preschool education policies across the world have therefore not only provided early education for vulnerable preschool children but importantly also activities for parents. Some intervention examples below:

Social learning Learning by interaction with, and observation of, others and copying what they do.

Social ecological This conceptualisation has social microsystems that directly or indirectly influence the child's development nested within each other like a Russian doll. Thus, the family microsystem is nested within the wider family system, and that is nested within the local community, and so on to local government, wider society and culture.

Transactional model Child development depends on a complex set of continuous dynamic interactional factors that occur reciprocally between the child and its social context, each influencing the other.

Perry Preschool Project intergenerational outcomes The iconic Perry Preschool Project in Michigan was a pioneering attempt in 1960s USA to address social mobility by eradicating disadvantage in vulnerable young children who were living in poverty and already at risk of failure. It was common practice then in USA to have children repeat the school year if they hadn't made sufficient progress so avoiding this was one of the aims of the Perry project. It took a Piagetian perspective with active learning and problem-solving central principles. It was a small-scale study of 123 disadvantaged African American children who were living in poverty. They were randomly allocated to the intervention group or the control group. The intervention group received high-quality preschool education each morning from qualified teachers for 2–3 years so that they were beginning their education earlier to give them a start before the age of formal schooling. Teachers also made a weekly home visit to involve the mothers in their children's education. The focus of this programme was specifically on education. You will see that later programmes discussed below were influenced by the Perry project but with remits broader than child education and parent support for their child's education.

Longitudinal research on the Perry project has collected data each year from the children who took part in the programme in the 1960s, now middle-aged adults. Initially, they showed improved school readiness as intended, but disappointingly this advantage seemed to fade by age seven. However, as participants grew older, interesting non-academic sleeper life cycle effects beyond the initial aims of school readiness were reported and are even passed on to Perry participants' children, now in their twenties. Participants in the intervention programme benefited from greater marriage stability, higher earnings, and less involvement with the criminal justice system, leading to better environments for rearing their children. Their children are less likely to be suspended from school, more likely to be in good health and in employment, less likely to be divorced (García et al., 2023; Muennig et al., 2009).

Project Headstart This started as a summer programme of compensatory preschool education with similar aims to the Perry project. Headstart was part of US President Lyndon Johnson's 'War on Poverty'. Congress then decided to extend it to full-time programmes in over 2500 communities across the USA that operated in various ways to be sensitive to local community culture and ethnicity. In 1973, Head Start added a home visiting element to the child education programme for intensive work with parents on enhancing parenting skills, emphasising parental involvement in their children's education and building effective parent–professional relationships. Its goals were broader than the Perry project which aimed to address mainly child educational goals. Headstart's two-generational approach is based on Bronfenbrenner's (1979) nested systems model (see Chapter 4). Recognising the importance of the early years for children's development, Early Headstart was introduced in 1995 to provide parental support from birth. Headstart and Early Headstart continue to run in the US to this day, as free, federally funded programmes. Their approach subsequently influenced policy on service delivery of early years interventions programmes outside the USA, for example, Sure Start in England, and Scotland, Wales, and Northern Ireland all had their own versions.

The Incredible Years programme This was developed in 1997 by Carolyn Webster-Stratton and now runs in 26 countries over six continents, including UK, Spain, Norway, and Canada. It aims to improve parenting skills and help children's all-round development and to help parents and children deal with disruptive and aggressive child behaviour, either preventive or targeted. It comprises four different parent training programmes aligned with different child ages – baby, toddler, preschool, and school-aged. Programmes run for 9–22 weeks. Influenced by Bandura's (1977) theory of social learning and modelling behaviour, the programme makes extensive use of video material to demonstrate parenting skills and stimulate discussion.

Online resource 11.3 Overview of Incredible Years programme
The Incredible Years (2013). Carolyn Webster-Stratton PhD annual faculty lecture 2006. 12 Feb. Available at: www.youtube.com/watch?v=FCmikgiL5zQ (Accessed: 28 February 2025).

Triple P – Positive Parenting Programme

This was developed in Queensland Australia and is delivered in many countries. This evidence-based programme was developed in recognition of the important influence of family risk factors on children's development. It started off as a small-scale home-based programme to support parents of disruptive preschoolers and has grown in scale into a public health intervention to prevent severe emotional, behavioural, and developmental problems in children and adolescents by enhancing parental child-rearing skills (Sanders, 2008). The central goal of Triple P is to enhance self-regulation for programme participants, parents, and children. It is underpinned by Bandura's social learning theory.

Online resource 11.4 Overview of Triple P programme
UQ Health (2019). The power of positive parenting. 26 June. Available at: www.youtube.com/watch?v=PtmOevzmg88 (Accessed: 28 February 2025).

Shonkoff (2010) argues that early intervention programme effects are positive but modest and that we need to look now towards ensuring that new scientific knowledge is incorporated in these programmes. In particular, he proposes that policy needs to build on evidence-based interventions and take account of what neuroscience now knows about the effects on brain development of growing up in stressful, adverse conditions, to construct new theories of developmental change. The next generation of early intervention programmes needs to implement a biodevelopmental framework in their planning with psychologists, educators, and health workers working together in an integrated, less fragmented way for the benefit of the most vulnerable children and their families who because of their multiple social problems, benefit least from current programmes. In Chapter 4, a similar point was made about the need for a shared model that better supports inter-professional collaboration.

We'll examine the relationship between research and policy further in the final chapter.

Summary

Chapter 11 focused on policy and practice underpinned by educational psychology to address three specific challenges for countries and school districts. National polices and guidelines for practice discussed in this chapter are examples of Bronfenbrenner's exosystems in that here there are systems outside the child and outside the school and home that have an impact on the child's development. The challenges examined in this chapter were that of supporting children with SEND, early intervention for disadvantaged preschoolers, and improving early literacy.

References/Further reading

Ajzen, I. (1991). The theory of planned behavior. *Organizational Behavior and Human Decision Processes*, *50*(2), 179–211.

Appleyard, K., Egeland, B., van Dulmen, M. H. M., & Alan Sroufe, L. (2005). When more is not better: The role of cumulative risk in child behavior outcomes. *Journal of Child Psychology and Psychiatry*, *46*(3), 235–245. https://doi.org/https://doi.org/10.1111/j.1469-7610.2004.00351.x

Bandura, A., & Walters, R. H. (1977). *Social learning theory* (Vol. 1). Prentice Hall.

Bond, G. L., & Dykstra, R. (1967). The cooperative research program in first-grade reading instruction. *Reading Research Quarterly*, *2*(4), 5–142.

BPS DECP (2022). The role of educational psychology in promoting inclusive education. *Position paper by Division of Educational and Child Psychology*. British Psychological Society.

Bronfenbrenner, U. (1979). *The ecology of human development: Experiments by nature and design*. Harvard University Press.

Brooks, G. (2023). Disputing recent attempts to reject the evidence in favour of systematic phonics instruction. *Review of Education*, *11*(2), e3408.

Davies, S., Janus, M., Duku, E., & Gaskin, A. (2016). Using the Early Development Instrument to examine cognitive and non-cognitive school readiness and elementary student achievement. *Early Childhood Research Quarterly*, *35*, 63–75.

Dell'Anna, S., Pellegrini, M., Ianes, D., & Vivanet, G. (2022). Learning, social, and psychological outcomes of students with moderate, severe, and complex disabilities inclusive education: A systematic review.

International Journal of Disability, Development and Education, *69*(6), 2025–2041. https://doi.org/10.1080/1034912X.2020.1843143

DfE (2023). *Educational psychology services: Workforce insights and school perspectives on impact.* Department for Education.

Ehri, L. C. (2020). The science of learning to read words: A case for systematic phonics instruction. *Reading Research Quarterly*, *55*(S1), S45–S60. https://doi.org/https://doi.org/10.1002/rrq.334

Ehri, L. C., Nunes, S. R., Stahl, S. A., & Willows, D. M. (2001). Systematic phonics instruction helps students learn to read: Evidence from the National Reading Panel's meta-analysis. *Review of Educational Research*, *71*(3), 393–447.

Ehri, L. C., Nunes, S. R., Willows, D. M., Schuster, B. V., Yaghoub-Zadeh, Z., & Shanahan, T. (2001). Phonemic awareness instruction helps children learn to read: Evidence from the national reading panel's meta-analysis. *Reading Research Quarterly*, *36*(3), 250–287. https://doi.org/https://doi.org/10.1598/RRQ.36.3.2

Freppon, P. A., & Dahl, K. L. (1998). Balanced Instruction: Insights and Considerations. *Reading Research Quarterly*, *33*(2), 240–251. https://doi.org/https://doi.org/10.1598/RRQ.33.2.5

García, J. L., Heckman, J. J., & Ronda, V. (2023). The lasting effects of early-childhood education on promoting the skills and social mobility of disadvantaged African Americans and their children. *Journal of Political Economy*, *131*(6), 1477–1506. https://doi.org/10.1086/722936

Glazzard, J. (2017). Assessing reading development through systematic synthetic phonics. *English in Education*, *51*(1), 44–57.

Glazzard, J., & Stones, S. (2020). A rigorous approach to the teaching of reading? Systematic synthetic phonics in initial teacher education. *Frontiers in Education*, *5*, 587155.

Goswami, U., & Bryant, P. (2016). *Phonological skills and learning to read.* Routledge.

Guralnick, M. J. (2006). Family influences on early development: Integrating the science of normative development, risk and disability, and intervention. In K. McCartney & D. Philips (Eds.), *Handbook of early childhood development* (pp. 44–61). Blackwell.

Hatcher, P. J., Hulme, C., & Snowling, M. J. (2004). Explicit phoneme training combined with phonic reading instruction helps young children at risk of reading failure. *Journal of Child Psychology and Psychiatry*, *45*(2), 338–358. https://doi.org/https://doi.org/10.1111/j.1469-7610.2004.00225.x

Isos Partnership (2024). *Towards an effective and financially sustainable approach to SEND in England.* Local Government Association.

Johnston, R. S., & Watson, J. E. (2004). Accelerating the development of reading, spelling and phonemic awareness skills in initial readers. *Reading and Writing*, *17*, 327–357.

Johnston, R. S., & Watson, J. E. (2005). *The effects of synthetic phonics teaching on reading and spelling attainment: A seven year longitudinal study* (Vol. 11). Scottish Executive Edinburgh.

Landerl, K. (2000). Influences of orthographic consistency and reading instruction on the development of nonword reading skills. *European Journal of Psychology of Education*, *15*, 239–257.

Luthar, S. S., Cicchetti, D., & Becker, B. (2000). The construct of resilience: A critical evaluation and guidelines for future work. *Child Development*, *71*(3), 543–562.

MacFarlane, K., & Marks Woolfson, L. (2013). Teacher attitudes and behavior toward the inclusion of children with social, emotional and behavioral difficulties in mainstream schools: An application of the theory of planned behavior. *Teaching and Teacher Education*, *29*(0), 46–52. https://doi.org/http://dx.doi.org/10.1016/j.tate.2012.08.006

Marks Woolfson, L. (2011). *Educational psychology: The impact of psychological research on education*. Pearson.

Marks Woolfson, L. (2024). Is inclusive education for children with special educational needs and disabilities an impossible dream? *British Journal of Educational Psychology*. https://doi.org/https://doi.org/10.1111/bjep.12701

Marks Woolfson, L., Geddes, R., McNicol, S., Booth, J. N., & Frank, J. (2013). A cross-sectional pilot study of the Scottish early development instrument: A tool for addressing inequality. *BMC Public Health*, *13*, Article 1187. https://doi.org/10.1186/1471-2458-13-1187

Muennig, P., Schweinhart, L., Montie, J., & Neidell, M. (2009). Effects of a prekindergarten educational intervention on adult health: 37-year follow-up results of a randomized controlled trial. *American Journal of Public Health*, *99*(8), 1431–1437.

Picton, I., Moisi, I., Jackson, T., & Clark, C. (2024). *Parents' support for young children's literacy at home in 2024*. National Literacy Trust.

Reinking, D., Hruby, G. G., & Risko, V. J. (2023). Legislating phonics: Settled science or political polemics? *Teachers College Record*, *125*(1), 104–131.

Ruijs, N., & Peetsma, T. (2009). Effects of inclusion on students with and without special educational needs reviewed. *Educational Research Review*, *4*, 67–79.

Rutter, M. (2013). Annual research review: Resilience–clinical implications. *Journal of Child Psychology and Psychiatry*, *54*(4), 474–487.

Ryan, R., Fauth, R., & Brooks-Gunn, J. (2013). Childhood poverty: Implications for school readiness and early childhood education.

In B. Spodek & O. Saracho (Eds.), *Handbook of research on early childhood education* (2nd ed., pp. 323–346). Erlbaum.

Sameroff, A. (2009). *The transactional model.* American Psychological Association.

Sameroff, A. (2010). A unified theory of development: A dialectic integration of nature and nurture. *Child Development*, *81*(1), 6–22.

Sanders, M. R. (2008). Triple P-Positive Parenting Program as a public health approach to strengthening parenting. *Journal of Family Psychology*, *22*(4), 506–517. https://doi.org/10.1037/0893-3200.22.3.506

Shonkoff, J. P. (2010). Building a new biodevelopmental framework to guide the future of early childhood policy. *Child Development*, *81*(1), 357–367.

Sohn, E. (2024). There's a strong push for more school psychologists. In *Trends Report. Monitor on Psychology* (Vol. 55). American Psychological Association.

Solity, J., & Vousden, J. (2009). Real books vs reading schemes: A new perspective from instructional psychology. *Educational Psychology*, *29*(4), 469–511. https://doi.org/10.1080/01443410903103657

Torgerson, C., Brooks, G., Gascoine, L., & Higgins, S. (2019). Phonics: Reading policy and the evidence of effectiveness from a systematic 'tertiary' review. *Research Papers in Education*, *34*(2), 208–238.

UK Parliament Public Accounts Committee. (2025). *Support for children and young people with special educational needs.* UK House of Commons. https://publications.parliament.uk/pa/cm5901/cmselect/cmpubacc/353/report.html

Urton, K., Wilbert, J., Krull, J., & Hennemann, T. (2023). Factors explaining teachers' intention to implement inclusive practices in the classroom: Indications based on the theory of planned behaviour. *Teaching and Teacher Education*, *132*, 104225.

Wilson, C., Marks Woolfson, L., Durkin, K., & Elliott, M. A. (2016). The impact of social cognitive and personality factors on teachers' reported inclusive behaviour. *British Journal of Educational Psychology*, *86*(3), 461–480.

Wyse, D., & Bradbury, A. (2022). Reading wars or reading reconciliation? A critical examination of robust research evidence, curriculum policy and teachers' practices for teaching phonics and reading. *Review of Education*, *10*(1), e3314. https://doi.org/https://doi.org/10.1002/rev3.3314

Wyse, D., & Goswami, U. (2008). Synthetic phonics and the teaching of reading. *British Educational Research Journal*, *34*(6), 691–710.

Yan, Z., & Sin, K.-f. (2014). Inclusive education: Teachers' intentions and behaviour analysed from the viewpoint of the theory of planned behaviour. *International Journal of Inclusive Education*, *18*(1), 72–85.

Section 5

Key emerging areas

This section in summary

Chapter 12

- Mental health and wellbeing
- Educational psychology for the good of society
- Narrowing the research-practice gap

DOI: 10.4324/9781032691541-16

Chapter 12

Where is educational psychology research headed?

In this final chapter, we explore emerging areas that present current challenges to society and that require a strategic pivot for educational psychology research. We examine ways to facilitate the translation of research findings into day-to-day practice that might help policy makers and practitioners make better use of both existing and future research.

Mental health and wellbeing

Educational psychology has mainly focused on academic learning and social behaviour. Regarding the latter, there has traditionally been a significant emphasis on interventions to manage externalising behaviours such as antisocial, aggressive, defiant, and impulsive behaviours which can be highly problematic in a classroom setting. Accordingly, there has been less emphasis in educational psychology on interventions for internalising behaviours such as depression and anxiety. A pressing need for this came to the fore when children returned to school post-COVID-19 (see Chapter 10). The Children's Society in 2024 reported a decline in children's mental health and wellbeing in the UK. NHS England's 2022 survey reported 1 in 5 young people aged 8–25 years as probably having a mental disorder, with possible eating disorders identified in 12% of 17–19-year-olds (Newlove-Delgado et al., 2022). Children's mental health services are struggling to offer the required support with long waiting lists. Educational psychology has a key role to play here researching evidence-based, universal, and preventive mental health programmes that can be delivered

DOI: 10.4324/9781032691541-17

within school curricula to build coping, problem-solving, and social skills for all children.

Educational psychology research for the good of society

Chapter 11 looked at the impact of educational psychology research on three big issues where policy and practice are determined at the level of Bronfenbrenner's **exosystem**, inclusive education, early intervention, and teaching young readers. Future educational psychology research may need to turn its attention away from the classroom microsystem to influence policy on other emerging exosystem issues of societal concern such as young people's increased use of social media, support for young refugees from global conflicts, and strategies to help learners make best use of new technology such as artificial intelligence. Next-stage educational psychology research can examine these big topics, do so from a culturally sensitive perspective, recognising diversity and difference, and collaborating with researchers from other disciplines to make a significant contribution to knowledge. This research can then have a global influence on policymakers and practitioners in a broad range of areas concerning children and young people.

Exosystem Exosystems are systems beyond the child like the local school district or the government, whose policies affect the child's experience in school, but with whom the child has no direct contact.

Narrowing the research-practice gap

Whatever research topics educational psychology works on, the key issue is how to ensure findings are translated into practice. Medicine and other health professions have led in developing research-practice links by advocating evidence-based guidelines for practice (see Chapter 7). Education though has been slower to make use of research findings and take **evidence-based practice** on board, rather than relying on educators' own experiences and preferences, or advice from peers (Marks Woolfson, 2018). Recent research by Pegram et al. (2022) reported that the majority of teacher interventions are still sourced through anecdotal recommendations from colleagues. This tendency extends from individual classroom decisions to wider policy decisions by school district directors (Slavin, 2020).

Evidence-led practice/evidence-based practice Applying the best available research findings to educational planning, intervention, and evaluation, rather than relying only on personal experience, judgement and preference, or advice from colleagues.

Research-practice gap The gap between academic knowledge and what practitioners in the field routinely do.

Online resource 12.1 The research-practice gap

TEDx Talks (2024). Is our education system actually backed by research? Dr Matthew Courtney. 16 May. Available at: www.youtube.com/watch?v=6K0v_gFFON8 (Accessed: 28 February 2025).

It is worth noting that the research-practice gap is an issue in many fields, beyond educational psychology. Many disciplines recommend practitioners to keep up to date with research findings themselves but to what extent is this a realistic expectation? They often do not have access to academic journals which might be behind a paywall, nor do they have allocated time within their working day. They maybe even lack the necessary specialist skills for abstracting implications for practice from findings reported in research papers. It is the responsibility of researchers to engage more with practitioners in order to take their findings forward into the field.

Here are some ways forward for narrowing the research-practice gap.

Disseminate implications of findings to non-academic users

Researchers in university departments have traditionally focused on publishing their research in academic journals and sharing findings with academic colleagues at conferences as this is a key element not only in theory-building but also in personal career-building. But in recent years, many research funders now require that academic researchers identify end users of their work and disseminate their findings to these important non-academic audiences. This dissemination is a sub-element of **translational science,** a problem-solving process where research insights and findings are translated from the laboratory into interventions to deal with human problems in the real world (Leppin et al., 2020). It is a step towards helping educational professionals embed evidence-based practice more effectively into their day-to-day practice (Shernoff et al., 2017). It is particularly important that authors of **meta-analyses, systematic reviews,** and **randomised controlled trials** disseminate their findings to education professionals and

Translational science Problem-solving process where research insights and findings are translated from the laboratory into interventions to deal with human problems in the real world.

Meta-analysis Statistical method of systematically synthesising similar datasets from many studies on the same research question.

Systematic review Results from several studies on the same question are synthesised. Meta-analysis may be included as part of a systematic review.

Randomised controlled trial (RCT) Gold standard experimental design. Participants are allocated to intervention and comparison groups by a random chance process. This process is assumed to control for possible confounding variables equally across both groups so that group differences found after the intervention can be considered as due to the intervention itself.

policymakers because these are especially valuable findings from the top of the **hierarchy of evidence** (see Chapter 9).

Hierarchy of evidence This is a ranking of research designs that reflects decreasing threats to internal validity.

Research into implementation science

Classroom professionals, however, have often been sceptical about relying on evidence-based practices because they are aware that unfortunately there is no intervention that works for every child, for every educator, in every context (Cook & Odom, 2013). Scaling up from a carefully controlled, funded, small-scale research intervention systematically carried out by an enthusiastic research team can run into problems when it's embedded into the daily routine of less-than-ideal, real-world classrooms over the varied environments of a number of schools. Competing organisational challenges and curricular commitments, resourcing, sickness, staff training, ethos and culture that differ from the research team, and lack of enabling support can all affect optimal intervention delivery and intended outcomes (Klingner et al., 2013). This leads us to another sub-area of translational science (Leppin et al., 2020) that of **implementation science**, introduced in Chapter 9. This is where research is focused on understanding the practicalities of how new approaches that worked in one school in a study can be scaled up and introduced in more schools across the district, while still maintaining fidelity of intervention delivery as for the original small-scale study. Key drivers for studying the science of implementation can be grouped into three broad domains: organisational drivers, staff competence drivers, and leadership drivers (Blase et al., 2012). Implementation science needs to be a future focus for educational psychology research.

Implementation science Systematic study of barriers and facilitators in order to improve the uptake of evidence-based research findings into practice.

Challenge of incorporating new research

Furthermore, in order not to get stuck simply repeating the same methods over the years, we also need to go beyond implementing in our practice what we already know about child development and identify how to bring new scientific findings into policy and practice (Shonkoff, 2010). Educational neuroscience research (also known as mind, brain, and education) is a good example of exciting new knowledge that offers promise for educational psychology. Imaging research leads us to new understandings of neural activity in children's brains when they are engaged in cognitive tasks such as reading or memory activities (Goswami, 2006).

Online resource 12.2 Educational neuroscience
Learnus UK (2018). Learnus interview Professor Michael Thomas. 25 September. Available at: www.youtube.com/watch?v=YBus87lq1XU (Accessed: 28 February 2025).

Applying research findings from this field so that classroom teachers can make use of these fresh insights to better promote children's learning is not straightforward, however. Some argue that direct links cannot be made from the neuroscience lab to the classroom and that the pathway from neuroscience to education needs to pass through a series of steps where neuroscience findings are incorporated into understandings at the levels of **cognitive neuroscience**, underlying psychological mechanisms and learning theories (Tommerdahl, 2010). There is a danger that in aiming to adopt cutting-edge, scientific approaches for the benefit of learners, educators may be tempted to buy commercial learning packages that promise to be brain-based, but whose scientific foundations may be weak (Sylvan & Christodoulou, 2010). Some researchers are working directly with teachers, training them in neuroscience insights, and recognising misunderstandings (Kelleher & Whitman, 2018). Debunking **neuromyths,** such as

Cognitive neuroscience Study of the neural mechanisms underlying mental processes such as memory.

Neuromyths Mythologies about brain function that are widely believed in education and influence teaching and curriculum design.

learning styles, that are common in education is a necessary element of this training (Grospietsch & Lins, 2021). Or it may be that this complex new area is too much to expect teachers to take on board alongside all the other competing pressures on their time and that a new specialist education professional, a neuroeducator, is needed to take this forward, building new bridges between the relevant disciplines (Leisman, 2023).

Collaborate earlier

Currently, there is typically a one-way relationship where psychology identifies a problem, designs a study to investigate it, gains funding, and then recruits teachers to participate. Or even at a further stage in the research-to-practice process, where psychology develops theories and disseminates research findings and, as discussed above, has previously left it to classroom practitioners, the end users, to try to work out how they might apply this valuable new knowledge in their real-life classrooms. We can do better than this. Improved dissemination of findings for non-academic audiences as above is one method. Another is for next-stage educational psychology research to emerge from collaboration with classroom practitioners early in the research process to jointly identify problems that need solutions.

Blurring of researcher and practitioner roles

Tkachencko et al. (2017) introduced the idea of researching practitioners and researchers who are also practitioners. The scientist-practitioner (researching practitioner) is already a familiar concept within educational psychology, with research being part of the job remit for school psychologists in several countries (e.g. Woods & Bond, 2014). The idea though of someone who is primarily a researcher but who has a practice base is less common. This points to a productive integration of research and practice professionals who can identify real classroom problems for investigation and be committed and involved from the very beginning in planning and implementing solutions.

Summary

In this last chapter, we concerned ourselves with how to bring educational psychology research forward for the future so that it will have greater impact on educators' policy and practice for the benefit of children and young people in schools. This includes a shift in focus to new concerns and building new connections between researchers and practitioners and bridges between educational psychology researchers and the different disciplines to collaborate on researching the big challenges of society today.

References/Further reading

Blase, K. A., van Dyke, M., Fixsen, D. L., & Bailey, F. W. (2012). Key concepts, themes, and evidence for practitioners in educational psychology. In B. Kelly & D. Perkins (Eds.), *Handbook of implementation science for psychology in education* (pp. 13–34). Cambridge University Press.

Cook, B. G., & Odom, S. L. (2013). Evidence-based practices and implementation science in special education. *Exceptional Children*, *79*(2), 135–144.

Goswami, U. (2006). Neuroscience and education: From research to practice? *Nature Reviews Neuroscience*, *7*(5), 406–413.

Grospietsch, F., & Lins, I. (2021). Review on the prevalence and persistence of Neuromyths in education–where we stand and what is still needed. *Frontiers in Education*, *6*, 995752.

Kelleher, I., & Whitman, G. (2018). A bridge no longer too far: A case study of one school's exploration of the promise and possibilities of mind, brain, and education science for the future of education. *Mind, Brain, and Education*, *12*(4), 224–230. https://doi.org/https://doi.org/10.1111/mbe.12163

Klingner, J. K., Boardman, A. G., & Mcmaster, K. L. (2013). What does it take to scale up and sustain evidence-based practices? *Exceptional Children*, *79*(2), 195–211. https://doi.org/10.1177/0014402913079002061

Leisman, G. (2023). Neuroscience in education: A bridge too far or one that has yet to be built: Introduction to the "Brain goes to school". *Brain Sciences*, *13*(1), 40.

Leppin, A. L., Mahoney, J. E., Stevens, K. R., Bartels, S. J., Baldwin, L.-M., Dolor, R. J., ... Meissner, P. (2020). Situating dissemination and implementation sciences within and across the translational research spectrum. *Journal of Clinical and Translational Science*, *4*(3), 152–158. https://doi.org/10.1017/cts.2019.392

Marks Woolfson, L. (2018). Engaging with the research-to-practice challenge. *International Journal of School and Educational Psychology*, *6*(3), 149–150.

Newlove-Delgado, T., Marcheselli, F., Williams, T., Mandalia, D., Davis, J., McManus, S. ... Ford, T. (2022). *Mental health of children and young people in England, 2022-wave 3 follow up to the 2017 survey.* NHS-Digital.

Pegram, J., Watkins, R. C., Hoerger, M., & Hughes, J. C. (2022). Assessing the range and evidence-base of interventions in a cluster of schools. *Review of Education*, *10*(1), e3336. https://doi.org/https://doi.org/10.1002/rev3.3336

Shernoff, E. S., Bearman, S. K., & Kratochwill, T. R. (2017). Training the next generation of school psychologists to deliver evidence-based mental health practices: Current challenges and future directions. *School Psychology Review*, *46*(2), 219–232. https://doi.org/10.17105/SPR-2015-0118.V46.2

Shonkoff, J. P. (2010). Building a new biodevelopmental framework to guide the future of early childhood policy. *Child Development*, *81*(1), 357–367.

Slavin, R. E. (2020). How evidence-based reform will transform research and practice in education. *Educational Psychologist*, *55*(1), 21–31.

Sylvan, L. J., & Christodoulou, J. A. (2010). Understanding the role of neuroscience in brain based products: A guide for educators and consumers. *Mind, Brain, and Education*, *4*(1), 1–7.

Tkachenko, O., Hahn, H.-J., & Peterson, S. L. (2017). Research–practice gap in applied fields: An integrative literature review. *Human Resource Development Review*, *16*(3), 235–262. https://doi.org/10.1177/1534484317707562

Tommerdahl, J. (2010). A model for bridging the gap between neuroscience and education. *Oxford Review of Education*, *36*(1), 97–109. https://doi.org/10.1080/03054980903518936

Woods, K., & Bond, C. (2014). Linking regulation of practitioner school psychology and the United Nations Convention on the Rights of the Child: The need to build a bridge. *School Psychology International*, *35*(1), 67–84.

Index

Note: Page numbers in *italic* refers to Figures.

www.ingramcontent.com/pod-product-compliance
Lightning Source LLC
Chambersburg PA
CBHW070328270326
41926CB00017B/3805